The Origins of Postmodernity

PERRY ANDERSON

VERSO
London • New York

First published by Verso 1998
© Perry Anderson 1998
All rights reserved

Reprinted 1998

The moral rights of the author have been asserted

Verso
UK: 6 Meard Street, London W1V 3HR
USA: 180 Varick Street, New York NY 10014–4606

Verso is the imprint of New Left Books

ISBN 1–85984–222–4 (pbk)
ISBN 1–85984–864–8

British Library Cataloguing in Publication Data
A catalogue record for this book is available from the British Library

Library of Congress Cataloging-in-Publication Data
A catalog record for this book is available from the Library of Congress

Typeset by SetSystems Ltd, Saffron Walden
Printed by Biddles Ltd, Guildford and King's Lynn

The Origins of Postmodernity

Contents

Foreword

This essay started when I was asked to introduce a new collection of writings by Fredric Jameson, *The Cultural Turn*. In the event, it became too long for the purpose. In publishing it as a text by itself, however, I have not wanted to alter its form: it is best read in conjunction with the volume that inspired it. Although I have never written about a body of work that I did not, in one way or another, admire, an element of resistance was in the past always an ingredient in the impulse to do so. Intellectual admiration is in any case one thing, political sympathy another. This short book tries do something else, which I have always found difficult: to express a sense of the achievement of a thinker with whom, it might be said, I lack the safety of sufficient distance. I have no assurance that I have succeeded. But some larger debate around Jameson's work in general is overdue, and this attempt may at least help to encourage it.

The title of the text has a two-fold reference. The principal aim of the essay is to offer a more historical account of the origins of the idea of postmodernity than is currently available: one that tries to set its different sources more precisely in their spatial, political and intellectual settings, and with greater attention to temporal sequence – also topical focus – than has become customary. Only against this background, my argument goes, does the peculiar stamp of Jameson's contribution emerge in full relief. A secondary purpose is to suggest, more tentatively, some of the conditions that may have released the postmodern – not as idea, but as phenomenon. In part, these are comments that seek to revise an earlier attempt to sketch the premises of modernism in the previous *fin de siècle*, and in part they try to engage with the lively contemporary literature on these questions.

I would like to thank the help of the Wissenschaftskolleg, Berlin, where this work was completed, and its exceptional librarians; and express my debts generally to Tom Mertes and my students in Los Angeles.

Prodromes

Lima – Madrid – London

'Postmodernism' as term and idea supposes the currency of 'modernism'. Contrary to conventional expectation, both were born in a distant periphery rather than at the centre of the cultural system of the time: they come not from Europe or the United States, but from Hispanic America. We owe the coinage of 'modernism' as an aesthetic movement to a Nicaraguan poet, writing in a Guatemalan journal, of a literary encounter in Peru. Rubén Darío's initiation in 1890 of a self-conscious current that took the name of *modernismo* drew on successive French schools – romantic, parnassian, symbolist – for a 'declaration of cultural independence' from Spain that set in motion an emancipation from the past of Spanish letters themselves, in the cohort of the 1890's.[1] Where in English the notion of 'modernism' scarcely entered general usage before mid-century, in Spanish it was canonical a generation earlier. Here the backward pioneered the terms of metropolitan advance – much as in the nineteenth century, 'liberalism' was an invention of the Spanish rising against French occupation in the epoch of Napoleon, an exotic expression from Cádiz at home only much later in the drawing-rooms of Paris or London.

So too the idea of a 'postmodernism' first surfaced in the

---

[1] 'Ricardo Palma', *Obras Completas*, Vol 2, Madrid 1950, p. 19: 'the new spirit that animates a small, but proud and triumphant, group of writers and poets in Spanish America today: modernism'.

Hispanic inter-world of the 1930's, a generation before its appearance in England or America. It was a friend of Unamuno and Ortega, Federico de Onís, who struck off the term *postmodernismo*. He used it to describe a conservative reflux within modernism itself: one which sought refuge from its formidable lyrical challenge in a muted perfectionism of detail and ironic humour, whose most original feature was the newly authentic expression it afforded women. De Onís contrasted this pattern – short-lived, he thought – with its sequel, an *ultramodernismo* that intensified the radical impulses of modernism to a new pitch, in a series of avant-gardes that were now creating a 'rigorously contemporary poetry' of universal reach.[2] De Onís's famous anthology of Spanish-language poets, organized according to this schema, appeared in Madrid in 1934, as the Left took office in the Republic amid the count-down to the Civil War. Dedicated to Antonio Machado, its panorama of 'ultramodernism' ended with Lorca and Vallejo, Borges and Neruda.

Minted by De Onís, the idea of a 'postmodern' style passed into the vocabulary of Hispanophone criticism, if rarely used by subsequent writers with his precision;[3] but it remained without wider echo. It was not until some twenty years later that the term emerged in the Anglophone world, in a very different

---

[2] Federico de Onís, *Antología de la Poesía Española e Hispanoamericana (1882–1932)*, Madrid 1934, pp. xiii–xxiv. For De Onís's view of the specificity of Hispanophone modernism, whose representative thinkers he believed to be Martí and Unamuno, see 'Sobre el Concepto del Modernismo', *La Torre*, April–June 1953, pp. 95–103. There is a fine synthetic portrait of Darío himself in *Antología*, pp. 143–152. During the Civil War, friendship with Unamuno restrained De Onís, but his basic outlook can be found in his commemoration of Machado: 'Antonio Machado (1875–1939), *La Torre*, January–June 1964, p. 16; and for recollections of his stance at the time, see Aurelio Pego, 'Onís, el Hombre', *La Torre*, January–March 1968, pp. 95–96.

[3] The influence of this usage was not confined to the Spanish-speaking world, but extended to the Luso-Brazilian as well. See, for a curious example, Bezerra de Freitas, *Forma e Expressão no Romance Brasileiro – Do período colonial à época post-modernista*, Rio de Janeiro 1947, where Brazilian modernism is dated from the Semana de Arte Moderna in Sao Paulo in 1922, under the impact of futurism, and associated essentially with the rupture of Mario de Andrade, and postmodernism held to have set in with an indigenist reaction by the thirties: pp. 319–326, 344–346.

context – as an epochal rather than aesthetic category. In the first volume of his *Study of History*, also published in 1934, Arnold Toynbee argued that the concurrence of two powerful forces, Industrialism and Nationalism, had shaped the recent history of the West. Since the last quarter of the nineteenth century, however, they had entered into destructive contradiction with each other, as the international scale of industry burst the bounds of nationality, yet the contagion of nationalism itself spread downwards into ever smaller and less viable ethnic communities. The Great War had sprung from the conflict between these trends, making it unmistakeably clear that an age had opened in which national power could no longer be self-sufficient. It was the duty of historians to find a new horizon appropriate to the epoch, which could only be found at the higher level of civilizations, beyond the outworn category of nation-states.[4] This was the task Toynbee set himself in the six volumes of his *Study* published – but still incomplete – before 1939.

By the time he resumed publication fifteen years later, Toynbee's outlook had altered. The Second World War had vindicated his original inspiration – a deep hostility to nationalism, and guarded suspicion of industrialism. Decolonization, too, had confirmed Toynbee's sceptical view of Western imperialism. The periodization he had proposed twenty years earlier now took on clearer shape in his mind. In his eighth volume, published in 1954, Toynbee dubbed the epoch that had opened with the Franco-Prussian War the 'post-modern age'. But his definition of it remained essentially negative. 'Western communities became "modern"', he wrote, 'just as soon as they had succeeded in producing a bourgeoisie that was both numerous enough and competent enough to become the predominant element in society'.[5] By contrast, in the postmodern age this middle class was no longer in the saddle. Toynbee was less definite about what followed. But certainly the postmodern age was marked by two developments: the rise of an industrial working class in the West, and the bid of successive intelligentsias outside

[4] *A Study of History*, Vol 1, London 1934, pp. 12–15.
[5] *A Study of History*, Vol 8, p. 338.

the West to master the secrets of modernity and turn them against the West. Toynbee's most sustained reflections on the emergence of a postmodern epoch focused on the latter. His examples were Meiji Japan, Bolshevik Russia, Kemalist Turkey, and – just born – Maoist China.[6]

Toynbee was no particular admirer of the resultant regimes. But he was scathing of the hubristic illusions of the late imperial West. At the close of the nineteenth century, he wrote, 'an unprecedently prosperous and comfortable Western middle-class was taking it as a matter of course that the end of one age of one civilization's history was the end of History itself – at least as far as they and their kind were concerned. They were imagining that, for their benefit, a sane, safe, satisfactory Modern Life had miraculously come to stay as a timeless present'.[7] Completely awry in the epoch, 'in the United Kingdom, Germany and the Northern United States the complacency of a post-Modern Western bourgeoisie remained unshaken until the outbreak of the first post-Modern general war in A.D. 1914'.[8] Four decades later, confronted with the prospect of a third – nuclear – war, Toynbee decided that the very category of civilization, with which he had set out to rewrite the pattern of human development, had lost pertinence. In one sense, Western civilization – as the unbridled primacy of technology – had become universal, but as such promised only the mutual ruin of all. A global political authority, based on the hegemony of one power, was the condition of any safe passage out of the Cold War. But in the long run, only a new universal religion – which would necessarily be a syncretistic faith – could secure the future of the planet.

Shaanxi – Angkor – Yucatan

Toynbee's empirical shortcomings, and vatic conclusions, combined to isolate his work at a time when commitment to the battle against Communism was expected to be less nebulous.

[6] *A Study of History*, Vol 8, pp. 339–346.
[7] *A Study of History*, Vol 9, London 1954, p. 420.
[8] *A Study of History*, Vol 9, p. 421.

After initial polemics, it was quickly forgotten, and with it the claim that the twentieth century could already be described as a postmodern age. Such was not to be the case with the virtually contemporaneous – in point of fact, slightly earlier – origination of the term in North America. Charles Olson, writing to his fellow-poet Robert Creeley on return from Yucatan in the summer of 1951, started to speak of a 'post-modern world' that lay beyond the imperial age of the Discoveries and the Industrial Revolution. 'The first half of the twentieth century', he wrote soon afterwards, was 'the marshalling yard on which the modern was turned to what we have, the post-modern, or post-West'.[9] On 4 November 1952, the day Eisenhower was elected President, Olson – ostensibly supplying information for a biographical directory of *Twentieth Century Authors* – set down a lapidary manifesto, beginning with the words 'My shift is that I take it the present is prologue, not the past', and ending with a description of that ' "going live present" ' as 'post-modern, post-humanist, post-historic'.[10]

The sense of these terms came from a distinctive poetic project. Olson's background lay in the New Deal. Active in Roosevelt's fourth Presidential campaign as head of the Foreign Nationalities Division of the Democratic National Committee, Olson was wintering in Key West in early 1945 with fellow party officials after electoral victory, awaiting preferment in the new administration. There, suddenly changing the course of his life, he started to plan an epic entitled *West*, covering the whole history of the Occidental world from Gilgamesh – later Odysseus – to the American present, and wrote a poem, originally entitled *Telegram*, renouncing public office, though not political responsibility: 'the affairs of men remain a chief concern'. Returning to Washington, Olson wrote on Melville and defended Pound; and worked for Oskar Lange – a war-time

[9] Charles Olson and Robert Creeley, *The Complete Correspondence*, Vol 7, Santa Rosa 1987, pp. 75, 115, 241, letters dated 9/8/51, 20/8/51 and 3/10/51. The last is an extended statement Olson entitled 'The Law', where the act of nuclear terror ends the modern age. 'Quite recently a door went bang shut', Olson writes. 'Biochemistry is post-modern. And electronics is already a science of communication – the "human" is already the "image" of the computing machine': p. 234.

[10] *Twentieth Century Authors – First Supplement*, New York,1955, pp. 741–742.

friend, now Polish Ambassador to the UN – lobbying the administration for the new government in Warsaw. Shaken by the nuclear bombing of Hiroshima and Nagasaki, he opposed Truman's renomination as a delegate to the Democratic Convention in 1948.[11]

By the time he was ready to take up his epic theme, its compass had altered. In mid-48, he wrote in *Notes for the Proposition: Man is Prospective*: 'Space is the mark of new history, and the measure of work now afoot is the depth of the perception of space, both as space informs objects and as it contains, in antithesis to time, secrets of a humanitas eased out of contemporary narrows . . . Man as object, not man as mass or economic integer, is the buried seed in all formulations of collective action stemming from Marx. This seed, not its tactic which merely secures it votes or coups d'etat, is the secret of the power and claim of collectivism over men's minds. It is the grain in the pyramid, and if it is allowed any longer to rot unrecognized, collectivism will rot as it did in nazism and as capitalism has by a like antinomian law. (Add: the persisting failure to count what Asia will do to collectivism, the mere quantity of her people enough to move the earth, leaving aside the moral grace of such of her leaders as Nehru, Mao, Sjahrir)'.[12] Of these last, one was of especial moment to Olson. In 1944, liaising with the White House for the Office of War Information, he had been angered by the bias of US policy towards the KMT regime in China, and hostility to the Communist base in Yenan. After the war, two friends kept him in touch with Chinese developments: Jean Riboud, a young French banker active in the Resistance, now an associate of Cartier-Bresson in New York; and Robert Payne, an English writer of Malrauvian cast, lecturer in Kunming during the Sino-Japanese War and reporter from Yenan after it, whose diaries offer an indelible image of the moral collapse of Chiang Kai-shek's regime, and the rise of Mao's alternative to it on the eve of the Civil War.[13]

[11] See Tom Clark, *Charles Olson. The Allegory of a Poet's Life*, New York 1991, pp. 84–93, 107–112, 138.

[12] 'Notes for the Proposition: Man is Prospective', *boundary 2*, II, 1–2, Fall 1973–Winter 1974, pp. 2–3.

[13] Robert Payne, *Forever China*, New York 1945; *China Awake*, New York 1947.

On the last day of January 1949, after a peaceful siege, Communist troops marched into Beijing, completing the liberation of North-East China. Almost immediately, Olson started to compose a poem conceived as a response to Eliot's modernist masterpiece – in his own words, an *Anti-Wasteland*.[14] He finished a first draft before the PLA crossed the Yangtze. The poem was completed in the summer at Black Mountain. Shanghai had fallen, but Guangzhou and Chongqing were still under KMT control; the People's Republic had not yet been proclaimed. *The Kingfishers*, with its great monosyllabic exordium:

> What does not change / is the will to change

places the Chinese revolution not under the sign of the new, but of the ancient. The poem opens with the legend of Angkor Wat's trade in the blue-green plumage of the kingfisher and the enigma of Plutarch's rock at Delphi, intersecting Mao's report to the CCP – time and space in counter-pointed balance:

> I thought of the E on the stone, and of what Mao said
> 'la lumière
>   but the kingfisher
> 'de l'aurore
>   but the kingfisher flew west
> 'est devant nous!'
>   he got the color of his breast
>   from the heat of the setting sun!

The lyrical transfusion is brief: ornithology dispels the mythic attributes of the *Four Quartets*.

> The legends are
> legends. Dead, hung up, the kingfisher
> will not indicate a favoring wind,

---

[14] For Olson's manuscript note defining his poem against Eliot's, see George Butterwick's magisterial essay, 'Charles Olson's "The Kingfishers" and the Poetics of Change', *American Poetry*, VI, No 2, Winter 1989, pp. 56–57.

or avert the thunderbolt. Nor, by its nesting,
still the waters, with the new year, for seven days.

Away from any current, deep in the tunnel of a bank, the
westering bird creates a foul nest from the remains of its prey.
What is aerial and iridescent is nurtured in filth and darkness:

> On these rejectamenta
> (as they accumulate they form a cup-shaped
> structure) the young are born.
> And, as they are fed and grow, this
> nest of excrement, and decayed fish becomes
> a dripping fetid mass
> Mao concluded:
> nous devons
> nous lever
> et agir![15]

The poem, however, comprehensively persists:

> The light is in the east. Yes. And we must rise, act. Yet
> in the west, despite the apparent darkness (the whiteness
> which covers all) if you look, if you can bear, if you can,
> long enough
>
> as long as it was necessary for him, my guide
> to look into the yellow of that longest-lasting rose,
> so you must

For the original peoples of America once came from Asia, and
their civilizations – however sombre – were less brutal than
those of the Europeans who conquered them, leaving to their
descendants runes of a life still to be recovered. Echoing a line

[15] Mao's call forms the final words of his Report to the meeting of the Central
Committee of the CCP held on 25–28 December 1947 at Yangjiagou in Shaanxi.
See 'The Present Situation and Our Tasks', *Selected Works*, Vol 4, Beijing 1969,
p. 173. Olson cited them in the French translation of the speech passed to him by
Jean Riboud.

from Neruda's *Alturas de Macchu-Picchu*, translated a few months before –

Not one death but many,
not accumulation but change, the feed-back proves,
                                        the feed-back is
the law

– the poem ends with the search for a future hidden in grubs and ruins:

I pose you your question:

shall you uncover honey / where maggots are?
I hunt among stones

Olson's aesthetic manifesto, *Projective Verse*, appeared the following year. Its advocacy of open-field composition as a development of the objectivist line of Pound and Williams became his most influential statement. But the reception of it generally failed to respect the motto he adopted from Creeley – 'form is never more than an extension of content'[16] – to Olson's poetry itself. Few poets have been treated more formally since. In fact, Olson's themes make up a *complexio oppositorum* unlike any other. A fierce critic of rationalist humanism – 'that peculiar presumption by which western man has interposed himself between what he is as a creature of nature and those other creations of nature which we may, with no derogation, call objects'[17] – Olson could seem close to a Heideggerian sense of Being as primal integrity. Yet he treated automobiles as domestic familiars in his verse, and was the first poet to draw on Norbert Wiener's cybernetics. He was much attracted to ancient cultures, Mayan or pre-Socratic, regarding the birth of archaeology as a decisive progress in human knowledge, because it could help recover them. But he saw the future as a collective

[16] 'Projective Verse', *Selected Writings of Charles Olson*, edited by Robert Creeley, New York 1966, p. 16.
[17] 'Projective Verse', p. 24.

project of human self-determination – man as 'prospective'. Anaximander lay at one end of his imagination, Rimbaud at the other. A democrat and anti-fascist, Olson assumed the persona of Yeats to defend Pound from prison, and as a patriot produced perhaps the only unmystified poem on the US Civil War.[18] Contemporary revolution came from the East, but America was subjoined to Asia: the colours of dawn in China and of flight into the West reflected the light of a single orbit. The phrase Olson used to describe himself – 'after the dispersion, an archaeologist of morning' – catches most of these meanings.

It was here, then, that the elements for an affirmative conception of the postmodern were first assembled. In Olson, an aesthetic theory was linked to a prophetic history, with an agenda allying poetic innovation with political revolution in the classic tradition of the avant-gardes of pre-war Europe. The continuity with the original *Stimmung* of modernism, in an electric sense of the present as fraught with a momentous future, is striking. But no commensurate doctrine crystallized. Olson, who thought of himself as timorous, was interrogated by the FBI for suspect war-time associations in the early fifties. Black Mountain College, of which he was the last Principal, shut its doors in 1954. In the years of reaction, his poetry became more straggling and gnomic. The referent of the postmodern lapsed.

New York – Harvard – Chicago

By the end of the fifties, when the term reappeared, it had passed into other – more or less casual – hands, as a negative marker of what was *less*, not more, than modern. In 1959 C. Wright Mills and Irving Howe – not coincidentally: they belonged to a common milieu of the New York Left – both employed it in this sense. The sociologist, in more caustic fashion, used the term to denote an age in which the modern ideals of liberalism and socialism had all but collapsed, as

---

[18] *Anecdotes of the Late War*, which starts: 'the lethargic vs. violence as alternatives of each other/for los americanos', and ends: 'Grant didn't hurry./He just had the most.//More of the latter died.' Compare the well-meaning pieties of *For the Union Dead*.

reason and freedom parted company in a postmodern society of blind drift and empty conformity.[19] The critic, in milder tones, borrowed it to describe a contemporary fiction unable to sustain modernist tension with a surrounding society whose class divisions had become increasingly amorphous with post-war prosperity.[20] A year later Harry Levin, drawing on Toynbee's usage, gave the idea of postmodern forms a much sharper twist, to depict an epigone literature that had renounced the strenuous intellectual standards of modernism for a relaxed middle-brow synthesis – the sign of a new complicity between artist and bourgeois, at a suspect cross-roads between culture and commerce.[21] Here lay the beginnings of an unequivocally pejorative version of the postmodern.

In the sixties, it changed as – still largely – adventitious sign again. Half-way through the decade the critic Leslie Fiedler, temperamental antithesis of Levin, addressed a conference sponsored by the Congress of Cultural Freedom, set up by the CIA for work on the intellectual front of the Cold War. In this unlikely setting, he celebrated the emergence of a new sensibility among the younger generation in America, who were 'drop-outs from history' – cultural mutants whose values of nonchalance and disconnexion, hallucinogens and civil rights, were finding welcome expression in a fresh postmodern literature.[22]

---

[19] 'We are at the ending of what is called The Modern Age. Just as Antiquity was followed by several centuries of Oriental ascendancy, which Westerners provincially call the Dark Ages, so now The Modern Age is being succeeded by a postmodern period': C. Wright Mills, *The Sociological Imagination*, New York 1959, pp. 165–167.

[20] Irving Howe, 'Mass Society and Post-Modern Fiction', *Partisan Review*, Summer 1959, pp. 420–436; reprinted in *Decline of the New*, New York 1970, pp. 190–207, with a postscript. Howe's article, although it makes no reference to Mills's work, is clearly dependent on it, especially *White Collar*: see in particular his description of a 'mass society' that is 'half-welfare and half-garrison', in which 'coherent publics fall apart'.

[21] 'What was Modernism?', *The Massachusetts Review*, August 1960, pp. 609–630; reprinted in *Refractions*, New York 1966, pp. 271–295, with a prefatory note.

[22] 'The New Mutants', *Partisan Review*, Summer 1965, pp. 505–525; reprinted in *Collected Papers*, Vol 2, New York 1971, pp. 379–400. Howe, as might be expected, complained about this text in a querulous survey, 'The New York Intellectuals', *Commentary*, October 1968, p. 49; reprinted in *The Decline of the New*, pp. 260–261.

This, Fiedler later explained in *Playboy*, would cross classes and mix genres, repudiating the ironies and solemnities of modernism, not to speak of its distinctions between high and low, in an uninhibited return to the sentimental and burlesque. By 1969 Fiedler's rendition of the postmodern could be seen, in its claims of demotic emancipation and instinctual release, as offering a prudently depoliticized echo of the student insurgency of the time, otherwise scarcely to be attributed with indifference to history.[23] A similar refraction can be detected in the sociology of Amitai Etzioni, later famous for his preaching of moral community, whose book *The Active Society* – dedicated to his students at Columbia and Berkeley in the year of campus rebellion – presented a 'post-modern' period, datable from the end of the war, in which the power of big business and established elites was declining, and society could for the first time become a democracy that was 'master of itself'.[24] The inversion of the argument of *The Sociological Imagination* is all but complete.

But if the usages of Howe and Mills were reversed with disciplinary symmetry by Fiedler and Etzioni, all were still terminological improvisation or happenstance. Since the modern – aesthetic or historical – is always in principle what might be called a present-absolute, it creates a peculiar difficulty for the definition of any period beyond it, that would convert it to a relative past. In this sense, the makeshift of a simple prefix – denoting what comes after – is virtually inherent in the concept itself, one that could be more or less counted on in advance to recur wherever a stray need for a marker of temporal difference might be felt. Resort of this kind to the term 'postmodern' has always been of circumstantial significance. But theoretical development is another matter. The notion of the postmodern did not acquire any wider diffusion till the seventies.

[23] 'Cross the Border, Close the Gap', *Playboy*, December 1969, pp. 151, 230, 252–258; reprinted in *Collected Papers*, Vol 2, pp. 461–485.
[24] *The Active Society*, New York 1968, pp. vii, 528.

Crystallization

Athens – Cairo – Las Vegas

The real turning-point came with the appearance in fall 1972 at Binghamton of a journal expressly subtitled a *Journal of Postmodern Literature and Culture* – the review *boundary 2*. The legacy of Olson had re-surfaced. The key-note essay in the first issue, by David Antin, was entitled: 'Modernism and Post-Modernism: Approaching the Present in American Poetry'. Antin raked the whole canon running from Eliot and Tate to Auden and Lowell, with glancing fire even at Pound, as a surreptitiously provincial and regressive tradition, whose metrical-moral propensities had nothing to do with genuine international modernism – the line of Apollinaire, Marinetti, Khlebnikov, Lorca, József, Neruda – whose principle was dramatic collage. In post-war America, it was the Black Mountain poets, and above all Charles Olson, who had recovered its energies.[1] The vitality of the postmodern present, after the break-down of an enfeebled poetic orthodoxy in the sixties, owed everything to this example. A year later, *boundary 2* devoted a double-issue to 'Charles Olson: Reminiscences,

[1] 'The appearance of Olson and the Black Mountain poets was the beginning of the end for the Metaphysical Modernist tradition, which was by no means a "modernist" tradition but an anomaly peculiar to American and English poetry. It was the result of a collision of strongly anti-modernist and provincial sensibilities with the hybrid modernism of Pound and the purer modernism of Gertrude Stein and William Carlos Williams': *boundary 2*, I, No 1, p. 120. Antin took Olson's great 'As the Dead Prey Upon Us' as his emblem of the new poetics.

15

Essays, Reviews' – the first full-scale appreciation since his death.

It was this reception that for the first time stabilized the idea of the postmodern as a collective reference. In the process, however, it underwent an alteration. Olson's call for a projective literature beyond humanism was remembered and honoured. But his political attachment to an unbidden future beyond capitalism – the other side of Rimbaud's 'courage' saluted in *The Kingfishers* – passed out of sight. Not that *boundary 2* was devoid of radical impulse. Its creator, William Spanos, decided to found the journal as a result of his shock at US collusion with the Greek Junta, while a visiting teacher at the University of Athens. He later explained that 'at that time, "Modern" meant, literally, the Modernist literature that had precipitated the New Criticism and the New Criticism which had defined Modernism in its own autotelic terms'. In Athens he sensed 'a kind of complicity' between this established orthodoxy, in which he had been trained, and the callous officialdom he was witnessing. On returning to America, he conceived *boundary 2* as a break with both. At the height of the Vietnam War, his aim was to 'get literature back into the domain of the world', at a time of 'the most dramatic moment of American hegemony and its collapse', and to demonstrate that 'postmodernism is a kind of rejection, an attack, an undermining of the aesthetic formalism and conservative politics of the New Criticism'.[2]

But the course of the journal was never quite to coincide with its intention. Spanos's own resistance to the Nixon Presidency was not in doubt – he was locked up for a demonstration against it. But twenty years of Cold War had made the climate unpropitious for a fusion of cultural and political vision: Olson's unity was not retrieved. *Boundary 2* itself remained, in its editor's own retrospect, essentially a literary journal, marked by

[2] 'A Conversation with William Spanos', *boundary 2*, Summer 1990, pp. 1–3, 16–17. This interview, by Paul Bové – Spanos's successor as editor of the journal – is a fundamental document for a history of the idea of the postmodern. After speaking of his arrest in protest against the bombing of Cambodia, Spanos acknowledges that 'I didn't quite associate what I was doing as a citizen with my literary, critical perspective. I don't want to say that they were absolutely distinguished, but I wasn't self-conscious of the connections'.

an existentialism originally Sartrean in sympathy, and then increasingly drawn to Heidegger. The result was to inflect Olson's objectivism towards a Heideggerian metaphysics of Being, that in due course became a dominant strand in *boundary 2*. The intra-mundane space of the postmodern was thereby – so to speak – left vacant. It was soon, however, occupied by a lateral entrant. Among early contributors to the journal was Ihab Hassan, a critic who had published his first essay on postmodernism just before it was launched. An Egyptian by birth – son of an aristocratic governor between the wars, famous for repression of a nationalist demonstration against British tutelage[3] – and engineer by training, Hassan's original interest had lain in a high modernism pared to an expressive minimum: what he called a 'literature of silence', passing down from Kafka to Beckett. When he advanced the notion of postmodernism in 1971, however, Hassan subsumed this descent into a much wider spectrum of tendencies that either radicalized or refused leading traits of modernism: a configuration that extended to the visual arts, music, technology, and sensibility at large.[4]

An extensive enumeration of trends and artists followed, from Mailer to *Tel Quel*, Hippies to Conceptualism. Within a heterogeneous range, however, a core cluster was discernible. Three names recurred with special frequency: John Cage, Robert Rauschenberg and Buckminster Fuller. All of these were associated with Black Mountain College. Absent, on the other hand,

[3] In 1930 Ismael Sidky, backed by the Palace and the British, closed the Egyptian parliament. Riots broke out across the country and were met with force. Casualties were particularly heavy at El Mansura. 'By the day's end, six people lay dead in the streets, four students in their teens. No one counted the wounded ... I felt my loyalties torn between my father and his foes. Three years later, Mustafa el Nahas became prime minister of Egypt. My father was forced to resign': Ihab Hassan, *Out of Egypt. Scenes and Arguments of an Autobiography*, Carbondale 1986, pp. 46–48: in more than one way, a suggestive memoir. For an anguished eyewitness account of the massacre, seen as an eleven-year-old from a balcony above it, compare the very different memoir of the Egyptian feminist Latifa Zayyat: *The Search*, London 1996, pp. 41–43. The background to these events is set out by Jacques Berque, *L'Egypte – Impérialisme et Révolution*, Paris 1967, pp. 452–460.
[4] 'POSTmodernISM: a Paracritical Bibliography', *New Literary History*, Autumn 1971, pp. 5–30; reprinted with some small alterations in *The Postmodern Turn*, Ithaca 1987, pp. 25–45.

was Olson. His place was, as it were, occupied by a fourth figure – Marshall McLuhan. In this combination, the pivot was clearly Cage: close friend of Rauschenberg and Fuller, and warm admirer of McLuhan. Cage was also, of course, the leading aesthetician of silence; his composition *4/33'* famously exceeding the gesture of any wordless drama. When Hassan concluded his survey of the motley indices of postmodernism – running from Spaceship Earth to the Global Village, faction and happening, aleatory reduction and parodic extravaganza, impermanence and intermedia – and sought to synthesize them as so many 'anarchies of the spirit', playfully subverting the aloof verities of modernism, the composer was one of the very few artists who could plausibly be associated with most of the bill.

In subsequent essays, Hassan enlisted Foucault's notion of an epistemic break to suggest comparable shifts in science and philosophy, in the wake of Heisenberg or Nietzsche. In this vein, he argued that the underlying unity of the postmodern lay in 'the play of indeterminacy and immanence', whose originating genius in the arts had been Marcel Duchamp. The list of his successors included Ashbery, Barth, Barthelme and Pynchon in literature; Rauschenberg, Warhol, Tinguely in the visual arts. By 1980, Hassan had annexed virtually a complete roster of poststructuralist motifs into an elaborate taxonomy of the difference between postmodern and modern paradigms, and expanded his Gotha of practitioners yet further.[5] But a larger problem remained. Is postmodernism, he asked, 'only an artistic tendency or also a social phenomenon?', and 'if so, how are the various aspects of this phenomenon – psychological, philosophical, economic, political – joined or disjoined?'. To these questions, Hassan returned no coherent answer, though making one significant observation. 'Postmodernism, as a mode of literary change, could be distinguished from the older avant-gardes (Cubism, Futurism, Dadaism, Surrealism etc) as well as from modernism', he wrote. 'Neither Olympian and detached like the

---

[5] Respectively: 'Culture, Indeterminacy and Immanence: Margins of the (Postmodern) Age', *Humanities in Society*, No 1, Winter 1978, pp. 51–85, and 'The Question of Postmodernism', *Bucknell Review*, 1980, pp. 117–126; reprinted in *The Postmodern Turn*, pp. 46–83, and (revised as 'The Concept of Postmodernism') pp. 84–96.

latter nor Bohemian and fractious like the former, postmodernism suggests a different kind of accommodation between art
and society'.[6]

What kind? If the difference was to be explored, it would be
difficult to avoid politics. But here Hassan drew back. 'I confess
to some some distaste for ideological rage (the worst are now
full of passionate intensity *and* lack all conviction) and for the
hectoring of religious and secular dogmatists. I admit to a
certain ambivalence towards politics, which can overcrowd our
responses to both art and life'.[7] He was soon more specific
about his dislikes, attacking Marxist critics for submission to
'the iron yoke of ideology' in 'their concealed social determin-
ism, collectivist bias, distrust of aesthetic pleasure'. Preferable
by far, as a philosophy for postmodernity, was 'the bluff
tolerance and optative spirit of American pragmatism', above
all in the expansive, celebratory shape of William James, whose
pluralism offered ethical balm for current anxieties.[8] As for
politics, the old distinctions had lost virtually any meaning.
Terms like 'left and right, base and superstructure, production
and reproduction, materialism and idealism' had become 'nearly
unserviceable, except to perpetuate prejudice'.[9]

Hassan's construction of the postmodern, pioneering though
many of its perceptions were – he was the first to stretch it
across the arts, and to note wing-marks later widely accepted –
thus had a built-in limit: the move to the social was barred. This
was surely one reason why he withdrew from the field at the
end of the eighties. But there was another, internal to his
account of the arts themselves. Hassan's original commitment
was to exasperated forms of classic modernism – Duchamp or
Beckett: just what De Onís had presciently termed 'ultra-
modernism' in the thirties. When he started to explore the
cultural scene of the seventies, Hassan construed it predomi-
nantly through this prism. The strategic role fell to vanguards
traceable back to the matrix of Black Mountain. Such an

[6] 'The Question of Postmodernism', pp. 122–124; the last sentence does not appear
in the revised version published in *The Postmodern Turn*, pp. 89–91.
[7] 'Pluralism in Postmodern Perspective' (1986), in *The Postmodern Turn*, p. 178.
[8] *The Postmodern Turn*, pp. 203–205, 232.
[9] *The Postmodern Turn*, p. 227.

estimate had much to be said for it. But there was always another aspect of the view Hassan was trying to describe, that was far closer to the languid or decorative involution of modernist *élan* which De Onís had contrasted as 'postmodernism'. Warhol could stand as short-hand for this strand.

Hassan's original conspectus included it, if without emphasis. Over time, however, he sensed that this was perhaps the overall direction in which the postmodern was tending. At mid-decade, a design exhibition in the Grand Palais, *Styles 85*, displaying a vast array of postmodern objects 'from thumbtacks to yachts', led him to a certain revulsion: 'Walking through the bright farrago, hectares of *esprit*, parody, persiflage, I felt the smile on my lips freeze'.[10] When he came to write the introduction to his collected texts on the topic, *The Postmodern Turn* in 1987, he made it clear the title was also a kind of farewell: 'Postmodernism itself has changed, taken, as I see it, the wrong turn. Caught between ideological truculence and demystifying nugacity, caught in its own kitsch, postmodernism has become a kind of eclectic raillery, the refined prurience of our borrowed pleasures and trivial disbeliefs'.[11]

In the very reason why Hassan became disabused with the postmodern, however, lay the source of inspiration for the most prominent theorization of it to succeed his own. Ironically, it was the art to which he gave least attention that finally projected the term into the public domain at large. In 1972 Robert Venturi and his associates Denise Scott Brown and Steven Izenour published the architectural manifesto of the decade, *Learning from Las Vegas*. Venturi had already made his name with an elegant critique of the purist orthodoxy of the International Style in the age of Mies, invoking Mannerist, Baroque, Rococo and Edwardian masterpieces as alternative values for contemporary practice.[12] In the new book, he and his colleagues launched a much more iconoclastic attack on Modernism, in the name of the vital popular imagery of the gambling strip.

---

[10] *The Postmodern Turn.* p. 229.

[11] *The Postmodern Turn*, p. xvii.

[12] *Complexity and Contradiction in Architecture*, New York 1966: 'Architects can no longer afford to be intimidated by the puritanically moral language of orthodox Modern architecture' – 'More is not less': p. 16.

Here, they argued, was to be found a spectacular renewal of the historic association of architecture with painting, graphics and sculpture – an exuberant primacy of symbol over space – that Modernism had to its cost foresworn. It was time to return to Ruskin's dictum that architecture was the decoration of construction.

Delivered with an air of casual learning, the laid-back message of *Learning from Las Vegas* rested on premises that would have dumbfounded Ruskin. 'The commercial strip challenges the architect to take a positive, non-chip-on-the-shoulder view', Venturi and his colleagues wrote. 'Las Vegas's values are not questioned here. The morality of commercial advertising, gambling interests, and the competitive instinct is not at issue'.[13] Formal analysis of the joyous riot of signs in the desert sky did not necessarily preclude social judgement, but it did rule out one standpoint. 'Orthodox Modern architecture is progressive, if not revolutionary, utopian and puristic: it is dissatisfied with *existing* conditions'. But the architect's principal concern 'ought not to be with ought to be but with what is' and 'how to help improve it'.[14] Behind the modest neutrality of this agenda – 'whether society was right or wrong was not for us at that moment to argue' – lay a disarming opposition. Contrasting the planned monotony of modernist megastructures with the vigour and heterogeneity of spontaneous urban sprawl, *Learning from Las Vegas* summed up the dichotomy between them in a phrase: 'Building for Man' vs. 'Building for men (markets)'.[15] The simplicity of the parenthesis says everything. Here, spelt out with beguiling candour, was the new relationship between art and society Hassan surmised but failed to define.

Venturi's programme, expressly designed to supersede the modern, still lacked a name. It was not long coming. By 1974 the term 'postmodern' – anticipated a decade earlier by Pevsner, to castigate a weak historicism – had entered the art world in New York, where perhaps the first architect to use it was Venturi's student Robert Stern. But the critic who made its

[13] *Learning from Las Vegas*, Cambridge, Mass. 1972, p. 0 [sic].
[14] *Learning from Las Vegas*, pp. 0, 85.
[15] *Learning from Las Vegas*, p. 84.

fortune was Charles Jencks, the first edition of whose *Language of Post-modern Architecture* appeared in 1977. Much more polemical in his obsequy for modernism – allegedly consigned to oblivion in 1972, with the the demolition of a high-rise in the Mid-West – Jencks was at first also more critical than Venturi of American capitalism, and of the collusion between the two in the principal types of post-war building commission. But, while arguing the need for a broader semiotic range than Venturi had allowed, to include iconic as well as symbolic forms, his prescriptions were essentially based on the ideas of *Learning from Las Vegas* – inclusive variety, popular legibility, contextual sympathy. Despite his title, Jencks was initially hesitant about calling these values 'post-modern', since the term was – he confessed – 'evasive, fashionable and worst of all negative'.[16] His preferred architecture would be better described as 'radical eclecticism', even 'traditionalesque', and its only accomplished exemplar to date was Antonio Gaudí.

Within a year Jencks had changed his mind, fully adopting the idea of the postmodern and now theorizing its eclecticism as a style of 'double-coding': that is, an architecture employing a hybrid of modern and historicist syntax, and appealing both to educated taste and popular sensibility. It was this liberating mixture of new and old, high and low, which defined postmodernism as a movement, and assured it the future.[17] In 1980

---

[16] *The Language of Post-Modern Architecture*, New York 1977, p. 7. Prompted in part by the work of the Marxist critic Malcolm MacEwan, a colleague of Edward Thompson on *The New Reasoner*, at this stage Jencks offered a periodization of 'modes of architectural production' – mini-capitalist; welfare state capitalist; monopoly capitalist, or the new, all-pervasive dominance of the commercial developer. 'Several modern architects, in a desperate attempt to cheer themselves up, have decided that since this is an inevitable situation, it must also have its good points ... "Main Street is almost all right", according to Robert Venturi': pp. 11–12, 35.

[17] *The Language of Post-Modern Architecture*, revised and enlarged Edition, New York 1978, pp. 6–8: 'Modernism suffers from elitism. Post-Modernism is trying to get over that elitism', by reaching out 'towards the vernacular, towards tradition and the commercial slang of the street' – 'architecture, which has been on an enforced diet for fifty years, can only enjoy itself and grow stronger and deeper as a result'. Discussion of the Pre-Modernist Gaudí was dropped from the new version, on grounds of consistency.

Jencks helped organize the architectural section of the Venice Biennale mounted by Paolo Portoghesi, a flamboyant pioneer of postmodern practice, entitled 'The Presence of Past', which attracted wide international attention. By now Jencks had become a tireless enthusiast of the cause, and prolific taxonomer of its development.[18] His most significant move was to distinguish, early on, 'late modern' from 'post-modern' architecture. Dropping the claim that modernism had collapsed in the early seventies, Jencks conceded that its dynamic still survived, if in paroxysmic form, as an aesthetic of technological prowess increasingly detached from functional pretexts – but still impervious to the play of retrospect and allusion that marked postmodernism: Foster and Rogers as against Moore and Graves.[19] This was the architectural equivalent of the literature championed by Hassan – ultra-modernism.

Noting the parallel, Jencks reversed the opposition between De Onís's terms without qualms. No matter how productive it might seem – like the cross-bow in the first years of fire-arms – such ultra-modernism was historically a rearguard. It was postmodernism, its symbolic resources answering to the contemporary need for a new spirituality, as once the exuberant baroque of the Counter-Reformation had done, that represented the advanced art of the age. By the mid-eighties Jencks was celebrating the Post-Modern as a world civilization of plural tolerance and superabundant choice, that was 'making nonsense' of such outmoded polarities as 'left- and right-wing, capitalist and working class'. In a society where information now mattered more than production, 'there is no longer an artistic avant-garde', since 'there is no enemy to conquer' in the global electronic network. In the emancipated conditions of today's art, 'rather there are countless individuals in Tokyo, New York, Berlin, London, Milan and other world cities communicating and competing with each other, just as they are

---

[18] He would later claim that 'the response to my lectures and articles was so forceful and widespread that it created Post-Modernism as a social and architectural movement': *Post-Modernism: the New Classicism in Art and Architecture*, New York 1987, p. 29.

[19] *Late Modern Architecture*, New York 1980, pp. 10–30.

in the banking world'.[20] Out of their kaleidoscopic creations, it was to be hoped, might emerge 'a shared symbolic order of the kind that a religion provides'[21] – the ultimate agenda of postmodernism. In aesthetic cross-dress, Toynbee's syncretistic dream had returned.

Montreal – Paris

The architectural capture of the blazon of the postmodern, which can be dated from 1977–78, proved durable. The primary association of the term has ever since been with the newest forms of built space. But this shift was followed, all but immediately, by a further extension of its range, in an unexpected direction. The first philosophical work to adopt the notion was Jean-François Lyotard's *La Condition Postmoderne*, which appeared in Paris in 1979. Lyotard had acquired the term directly from Hassan. Three years earlier, he had addressed a conference at Milwaukee on the postmodern in the performing arts orchestrated by Hassan. Declaring 'the stakes of postmodernism as a whole' were 'not to exhibit truth within the closure of representation but to set up *perspectives* within the return of the *will*', Lyotard extolled Michael Snow's famous experimental film of an empty Canadian landscape scanned by an immobile swivelling camera, and Duchamp's spatial projections.[22] His new book was quite close to a theme in Hassan – the epistemological implications of recent advances in the natural sciences. The immediate occasion of *La Condition Postmoderne*, however, was a commission to produce a report on the state of 'contemporary knowledge' for the university council of the government of Quebec, where the nationalist party of René Levesque had just come to power.

For Lyotard, the arrival of postmodernity was linked to the

---

[20] *What is Post-Modernism?*, London 1986, pp. 44–47.

[21] *What is Post-Modernism?*, p. 43.

[22] 'The Unconscious as Mise-en-Scène', in Michael Benamou and Charles Caramello (eds), *Performance in Postmodern Culture*, Madison 1977, p. 95. Hassan gave the key-note address at this conference. For the intellectual contact between the two at this time, see *La Condition Postmoderne*, notes 1, 121, 188, and *The Postmodern Turn*, pp. 134, 162–164.

emergence of a post-industrial society – theorized by Daniel Bell and Alain Touraine – in which knowledge had become the main economic force of production in a flow by-passing national states, yet at the same time had lost its traditional legitimations. For if society was now best conceived, neither as an organic whole nor as a dualistic field of conflict (Parsons or Marx), but as a web of linguistic communications, language itself – 'the whole social bond' – was composed of a multiplicity of different games, whose rules were incommensurable, and inter-relations agonistic. In these conditions, science became just one language game among others: it could no longer claim the imperial privilege over other forms of knowledge to which it had pretended in modern times. In fact, its title to superiority as denotative truth over narrative styles of customary knowledge concealed the basis of its own legitimation, which classically rested on two forms of grand narrative itself. The first of these, derived from the French Revolution, told a tale of humanity as the heroic agent of its own liberation through the advance of knowledge; the second, descending from German Idealism, a tale of spirit as the progressive unfolding of truth. Such were the great justifying myths of modernity.

The defining trait of the postmodern condition, by contrast, is the loss of credibility of these meta-narratives. For Lyotard, they have been undone by the immanent development of the sciences themselves: on the one hand, by a pluralization of types of argument, with the proliferation of paradox and paralogism – anticipated within philosophy by Nietzsche, Wittgenstein and Levinas; and on the other hand, by a technification of proof, in which costly apparatuses, commanded by capital or the state, reduce 'truth' to 'performativity'. Science in the service of power finds a new legitimation in efficiency. But the genuine pragmatics of postmodern science lies not in the pursuit of the performative, but in the production of the paralogistic – in micro-physics, fractals, discoveries of chaos, 'theorizing its own evolution as discontinuous, catastrophic, nonrectifiable and paradoxical'.[23] If the dream of consensus is a relic of nostalgia for emancipation,

---

[23] *La Condition Postmoderne. Rapport sur le Savoir*, Paris 1979, p. 97. English translation: *The Postmodern Condition*, Minneapolis 1984, p. 60.

narratives as such do not disappear, but become miniature and competitive: 'the little narrative remains the quintessential form of imaginative invention'.[24] Its social analogue, on which *The Postmodern Condition* ends, is the trend towards the temporary contract in every area of human existence: occupational, emotional, sexual, political – ties more economical, flexible, creative than the bonds of modernity. If this form is favoured by the 'system', it is not entirely subject to it. We should be happy it is modest and mixed, Lyotard concluded, because any pure alternative to the system would fatally come to resemble what it sought to oppose.

At the turn of the seventies, Hassan's essays – essentially on literature – had still to be collected; Jencks's writing was limited to architecture. In title and topic, *The Postmodern Condition* was the first book to treat postmodernity as a general change of human circumstance. The vantage-point of the philosopher assured it a wider echo, across audiences, than any previous intervention: it remains to this day perhaps the most widely cited work on the subject. But taken in isolation – as it usually is – the book is a misleading guide to Lyotard's distinctive intellectual position. For *The Postmodern Condition*, written as an official commission, is confined essentially to the epistemological fate of the natural sciences – about which, as Lyotard later confessed, his knowledge was less than limited.[25] What he read into them was a cognitive pluralism, based on the notion – fresh to Gallic audiences, if long staled to Anglo-Saxon – of different, incommensurable language-games. The incoherence of Wittgenstein's original conception, often noted, was only compounded by Lyotard's claim that such games were both autarchic and agonistic, as if there could be conflict between what has no common measure. The subsequent influence of the book, in this sense, was in inverse relation to its intellectual interest, as it became the inspiration of a street-level relativism

---

[24] *La Condition Postmoderne*, p. 98; *The Postmodern Condition*, p. 60.

[25] 'I made up stories, I referred to a quantity of books I'd never read, apparently it impressed people, it's all a bit of parody ... It's simply the worst of my books, they're almost all bad, but that one's the worst': *Lotta Poetica*, Third Series, Vol 1, No 1, January 1987, p. 82 – an interview of more general biographical interest.

that often passes – in the eyes of friends and foes alike – for the hallmark of postmodernism.

What the ostensibly scientific framework of Lyotard's 'report on knowledge' left out of view was either the arts or politics. The curiosity of the book lay in the fact these were his two principal passions as a philosopher. A militant in the far-left group *Socialisme ou Barbarie* for a decade (1954–64) during which he was an outstandingly lucid commentator on the Algerian War, Lyotard remained active in its split-off *Pouvoir Ouvrier* for another two years. Breaking with this group when he became convinced the proletariat was no longer a revolutionary subject capable of challenging capitalism, he was active in the university ferment at Nanterre in 1968 and still reinterpreting Marx for contemporary rebels as late as 1969. But with the ebb of insurgency in France, Lyotard's ideas shifted. His first major philosophical work, *Discours, Figure* (1971), advanced a figural rendering of Freudian drives, in opposition to Lacan's linguistic account of the unconscious, as the basis for a theory of art, illustrated by poems and paintings.

By the time of *Dérive à partir de Marx et Freud* (1973), he had arrived at a more drastic political energetics. 'Reason', he declared, 'is already in power in kapital. We do not want to destroy kapital because it is not rational, but because it is. Reason and power are all one'. There was 'nothing in kapitalism, no dialectic that will lead to its supersession, its overcoming in socialism: socialism, it is now plain to all, is identical to kapitalism. All critique, far from surpassing, merely consolidates it.' What alone could destroy capitalism was the world-wide 'drift of desire' among the young, away from libidinal investment in the system, to styles of conduct 'whose sole guide is affective intensity and the multiplication of libidinal power'.[26] The role of advanced artists – once Opojaz, Futurism or LEF in Russia; today Rothko, Cage or Cunningham in America – was to blow up the obstacles to the unleashing of this desire by committing the forms of established reality to the flames. Art in this sense lay beneath all insurgent politics. 'Aesthetics has been for the political man I was (and remain?) not an alibi, a

[26] *Dérive à partir de Marx et Freud*, Paris 1973, pp. 12–13, 16–18.

27

comfortable retreat, but the fault and fissure to descend to the subsoil of the political scene, a vast grotto from which its underside can be seen upside-down or turned inside-out'.[27]

With *Economie Libidinale* (1974), Lyotard went a step further. No critique of Marx, by such *naïfs* as Castoriadis or Baudrillard, in the name of a pious cult of creativity or nostalgic myth of symbolic exchange, was of any avail. To unmask 'the desire named Marx', a complete transcription was needed of political into libidinal economy, that would not shrink from the truth that exploitation itself was typically lived – even by the early industrial workers – as erotic enjoyment: masochistic or hysterical delectation in the destruction of physical health in mines and factories, or disintegration of personal identity in anonymous slums. Capital was *desired* by those it dominated, then as now. Revolt against it came only when the pleasures it yielded became 'untenable', and there was an abrupt shift to new outlets. But these had nothing to do with the traditional sanctimonies of the Left. Just as there was no alienation involved in popular investment in capital, so in disinvestment 'there is no libidinal dignity, nor libidinal liberty, nor libidinal fraternity' – just the quest for new affective intensities.[28]

The larger background to Lyotard's transit from a revolutionary socialism towards a nihilist hedonism lay, of course, in the evolution of the Fifth Republic itself. The Gaullist consensus of the early sixties had convinced him that the working class was now essentially integrated into capitalism. The ferment of the late sixties gave him hope that generation rather than class – youth across the world – might be the harbinger of revolt. The euphoric wave of consumerism that washed over the country in the early and mid-seventies then led to (widespread) theorizations of capitalism as a stream-lined machinery of desire. By 1976, however, the Socialist and Communist Parties had agreed on a Common Programme, and looked increasingly likely to win the next legislative elections. The prospect of the PCF in government for the first time since the onset of the Cold War sowed panic in respectable opinion, prompting a violent ideo-

---

[27] *Dérive à partir de Marx et Freud*, p. 20.

[28] *Economie Libidinale*, Paris 1974, pp. 136–138.

logical counter-offensive. The result was the rocketing to prominence of the *Nouveaux Philosophes*, a group of former *soixante-huitard* publicists, patronized by the media and the Elysée.

In the vicissitudes of Lyotard's political trajectory, there had always been one constant. *Socialisme ou Barbarie* was vehemently anti-communist from the first, and whatever his other changes of mood or conviction, this remained an ineradicable element in his outlook. In 1974 he confided to startled friends in America that his Presidential choice was Giscard, since Mitterrand relied on Communist support. As the 1978 elections approached, with the danger of actual PCF participation in government, he therefore could not but feel ambivalence towards the *Nouveaux Philosophes*. On the one hand, their furious attacks on communism were salutary; on the other, they were visibly a light-weight coterie caught up in a compromising embrace with official power. Lyotard's intervention in the pre-electoral debates, the sardonic dialogue *Instructions Païennes* (1977), accordingly both defended and derided them. It was here that he first formulated the idea of meta-narratives that was to figure so prominently in *The Postmodern Condition*, and made its real target crystal-clear. Just one 'master narrative' lay at the origin of the term: Marxism. Fortunately, its ascendancy was now at last eroded by the innumerable little tidings from the Gulag. It was true that in the West there existed a grand narrative of capital too; but it was preferable to that of the Party, since it was 'godless' – 'capitalism has no respect for any one story', for 'its narrative is about everything and nothing'.[29]

In the same year as this political manifesto, Lyotard set out an aesthetic canon. *Les Transformateurs Duchamp* presented the creator of the *Large Glass* and *Given* as the critical artist of the non-isomorphic, of incongruences and incommensurabilities. Defending once again his account of the *jouissance* of the early industrial proletariat in its grinding lot, Lyotard contended:

---

[29] *Instructions Païennes*, Paris 1977, p. 55. Lyotard's first use of the terms 'grand narrative' and 'meta-narrative' identifies their referent without further ado as Marxism: pp. 22–23.

'If you describe the workers' fate exclusively in terms of alienation, exploitation and poverty, you present them as victims who only suffered passively the whole process and who only acquired claims for later reparations (socialism). You miss the essential, which isn't the growth of the forces of production at any price, nor even the death of many workers, as Marx often says with a cynicism adorned with Darwinism. You miss the energy that later spread through the arts and sciences, the jubilation and the pain of discovering that you can hold out (live, work, think, be affected) in a place where it had been judged senseless to do so. Indifferent to sense, hardness.' It was this hardness, a 'mechanical asceticism', of which Duchamp's sexual enigmas took a reading. 'The *Glass* is the "delay" of the nude; *Given* its advance. It's too soon to see the woman laying herself bare on the *Glass*, and it's too late on the stage of the *Given*. The performer is a complex *transformer*, a battery of metamorphosis machines. There is no art, because there are no objects. There are only transformations, redistributions of energy. The world is a multiplicity of apparatuses that transform units of energy into one other.'[30]

The immediate hinterland behind *The Postmodern Condition* was thus much more intensely charged than the document composed for the Québecois state itself. The 'report on knowledge' left the two questions of most abiding concern to Lyotard suspended. What were the implications of postmodernity for art and politics? Lyotard was quickly forced to reply to the first, where he found himself in an awkward position. When he wrote *The Postmodern Condition* he was quite unaware of the deployment of the term in architecture, perhaps the only art on which he had never written, with an aesthetic meaning antithetical to everything that he valued. This ignorance could not last long. By 1982 he was apprised of Jencks's construction of the postmodern, and its widespread reception in North America. His reaction was acrid. *Such* postmodernism was a surreptitious restoration of a degraded realism once patronized by Nazism and Stalinism and now recycled as a cynical eclecticism

---

[30] *Les Transformateurs Duchamp*, Paris 1977, pp. 23, 39–40.

by contemporary capital: everything the avant-gardes had fought against.[31]

What this slackening of aesthetic tension promised was not just the end of experimentation, but a cancellation of the impetus of modern art as such, whose drive had always come from the gap between the conceivable and the presentable, that Kant defined as the sublime as distinct from the merely beautiful. What then could authentic postmodern art be? Preempted by a usage he execrated, Lyotard's answer was lame. The postmodern did not come after the modern, but was a motion of internal renewal within it from the first – that current whose response to the shattering of the real was the opposite of nostalgia for its unity: rather a jubilant acceptance of the freedom of invention it released. But this was no luxuriance. The avant-garde art Lyotard singled out for approval a year later was Minimalism – the sublime as privation. What buoyed the art market, by contrast, was the kitsch celebrated by Jencks: 'amalgamation, ornamentation, pastiche – flattering the "taste" of a public that can have no taste'.[32]

If Lyotard's problem in theorizing a postmodern art lay in the turn of aesthetic trends away from the direction he had always championed – forcing him to declare artistic postmodernity a perennial principle, rather than periodic category, in patent contradiction of his account of scientific postmodernity as a stage of cognitive development – his difficulty in constructing a postmodern politics became in due course analogous. Here the discomfiture came from the course of history itself. In *The Postmodern Condition* Lyotard had announced the eclipse of all grand narratives. The one whose death he above all sought to certify was, of course, classical socialism. In subsequent texts, he would extend the list of grand narratives that were now defunct: Christian redemption, Enlightenment progress, Hegelian spirit, Romantic unity, Nazi racism, Keynesian equilibrium.

---

[31] 'Réponse à la question: qu'est-ce que le postmoderne?', in *Le Postmoderne expliqué aux enfants*, Paris 1986, pp. 29–33. English translation, 'Answering the Question: What is Postmodernism?', appended to *The Postmodern Condition*, pp. 73–76.
[32] 'Le sublime et l'avant-garde' (Berlin lecture 1983), in *L'Inhumain. Causeries sur le Temps*, Paris 1988, p. 117.

But the commanding referent always remained communism. What, then, of capitalism? At the time Lyotard was writing, at the tail-end of the Carter era, the West – then entering a severe recession – was in far from boisterous ideological mood. Hence he could suggest with at any rate a semblance of plausibility that contemporary capitalism was validated by no more than a performance principle, which was a mere shadow of real legitimation.

With the sharp change of conjuncture in the eighties – the euphoria of the Reagan boom, and the triumphant ideological offensive of the Right, culminating in the collapse of the Soviet bloc at the end of the decade – this position lost all credibility. Far from grand narratives having disappeared, it looked as if for the first time in history the world was falling under the sway of the most grandiose of all – a single, universal story of liberty and prosperity, the global victory of the market. How was Lyotard to adjust to this uncovenanted development? His initial reaction was to insist that capitalism, though it might seem to represent a universal finality of history, in fact destroyed any – since it embodied no higher values than mere factual security. 'Capital has no need for legitimation, it prescribes nothing, in the strict sense of an obligation, it does not have to post any normative rule. It is present everywhere, but as necessity rather than finality'. At best perhaps, it concealed a quasi-norm – 'saving time': but could that really be regarded as a universal end?[33]

This was an uncharacteristically weak note to strike. By the end of the nineties, Lyotard had found a stronger exit from his difficulty. Capitalism, he had started to argue much earlier, was not to be understood primarily as a socio-economic phenomenon at all. 'Capitalism is, more properly, a figure. As a system, capitalism has as its heat source not the labour force but energy itself, physics (the system is not isolated). As figure, capitalism derives its force from the Idea of infinity. It can appear in human experience as the desire for money, the desire for power, or the desire for novelty. All this can seem very ugly, very

---

[33] 'Mémorandum sur la légitimité' (1984), in *Le Postmoderne expliqué aux enfants*, p. 94.

disquieting. But these desires are the anthropological translation of something that is ontologically the "instantiation" of infinity in the will. This "instantiation" does not take place according to social class. Social classes are not pertinent ontological categories'.[34] The substitution of history by ontology was a way-station, however: within a few years, Lyotard had moved to astro-physics.

The triumph of capitalism over rival systems, he now argued, was the outcome of a process of natural selection that pre-dated human life itself. In the incommensurable vastness of the cosmos, where all bodies are subject to entropy, an aboriginal chance – a 'contingent constellation of energy forms' – gave rise in one tiny planet to rudimentary living systems. Because external energy was limited, these had to compete with each other, in a perpetually fortuitous path of evolution. Eventually, after millions of years, a human species emerged capable of words and tools; then 'various improbable forms of human aggregation arose, and they were selected according to their ability to discover, capture and save sources of energy'. After further millennia, punctuated by the neolithic and industrial revolutions, 'systems called liberal democracies' proved themselves best at this task, trouncing communist or islamist competitors, and moderating ecological dangers. 'Nothing seemed able to stop the development of this system except the ineluctable extinction of the sun. But to meet this challenge, the system was already developing the prostheses that would allow it to survive after solar sources of energy were wiped out'.[35] All contemporary scientific research was ultimately working towards the exodus, four billion years hence, of a transformed human species from the earth.

When first adumbrating this vision, Lyotard termed it a 'new décor'.[36] Resort to the language of scenography side-stepped any hint of narrative – if at the cost of unwittingly suggesting the stylization of the postmodern otherwise most disliked. But

---

[34] 'Appendice svelte à la question postmoderne' (1982), in *Tombeau de l'intellectuel et autres papiers*, Paris 1984, p. 80.

[35] *Moralités Postmodernes*, Paris 1993, pp. 80–86.

[36] 'Billet pour un nouveau décor' (1985), in *Le Postmoderne expliqué aux enfants*, pp. 131–134.

when completed, he presented it as 'the unavowed dream the postmodern world dreams about itself' – 'a postmodern fable'. But, he insists, 'the fable is realistic because it recounts the story of a force which makes, unmakes and remakes reality'. What the fable depicts is a conflict between two energy processes. 'One leads to the destruction of all systems, all bodies, living or not, on our planet and the solar system. But within this process of entropy, which is necessary and continuous, another process that is contingent and discontinuous, at least for a long time, acts in a contrary sense by increasing differentiation of its systems. This movement cannot halt the first (unless it could find a means to refuel the sun), but it can escape from catastrophe by abandoning its cosmic habitat'. The ultimate motor of capitalism is thus not thirst for profit, or any human desire: it is rather development as neguentropy. 'Development is not an invention of human beings. Human beings are an invention of development'.[37]

Why is this not a – quintessentially modern – grand narrative? Because, Lyotard maintains, it is a story without historicity or hope. The fable is postmodern because 'it has no finality in any horizon of emancipation'. Human beings, as witnesses of development, may set their faces against a process of which they are vehicles. 'But even their critiques of development, of its inequality, its irregularity, its fatality, its inhumanity, are expressions of development and contribute to it.' Universal energetics leaves no space for pathos – ostensibly. Yet Lyotard also freely describes his story as a 'tragedy of energy' which 'like *Oedipus Rex* ends badly', yet also 'like *Oedipus at Colonnus* allows an ultimate remission'.[38]

The intellectual fragility of this late construction hardly needs emphasis. Nothing in Lyotard's original account of meta-narratives confined them to the idea of emancipation – which was only one of the two modern discourses of legitimation he sought to trace. The postmodern fable would still be a grand narrative, even were it exempt from the theme. But in fact, of course, it is not. What else would escape to the stars be than

[37] 'Une fable postmoderne', in *Moralités Postmodernes*, pp. 86–87.
[38] 'Une fable postmoderne', pp. 91–93, 87.

emancipation from the bounds of a dying earth? More pointedly still, in the other – interchangeable – register of Lyotard's narrative, capitalism notoriously speaks the language of emancipation more continually and confidently than ever before. Elsewhere, Lyotard is forced to acknowledge this. Indeed, he admits: 'Emancipation is no longer the task of gaining and imposing liberty from the outside' – rather it is 'an ideal that the system itself endeavours to actualize in most of the areas it covers, such as work, taxation, marketplace, family, sex, race, school, culture, communication'. Obstacles and resistances only encourage it to become more open and complex, promoting spontaneous undertakings – and 'that is tangible emancipation'. If the job of the critic is still to denounce the shortcomings of the system, 'such critiques, whatever form they take, are needed by the system for discharging the task of emancipation more effectively'.[39]

The postmodern condition, announced as the death of grand narrative, thus ends with its all but immortal resurrection in the allegory of development. The logic of this strange dénouement is inscribed in Lyotard's political trajectory. From the seventies onwards, so long as communism existed as an alternative to capitalism, the latter was a lesser evil – he could even sardonically celebrate it as, by contrast, a pleasurable order. Once the Soviet bloc had disintegrated, the hegemony of capital became less palatable. Its ideological triumph appeared to vindicate just the kind of legitimating narrative whose obituary Lyotard had set out to write. Rather than confronting the new reality on a political plane, his solution was a metaphysical sublimation of it. Suitably projected into inter-galactic space, his original energetics could put capitalism into perspective as no more than an eddy of a larger cosmic adventure. The bitter-sweet consolation this alteration of scale might offer a former militant is clear. The 'postmodern fable' did not spell any final reconciliation with capital. On the contrary, Lyotard now recovered accents of opposition long muted in his work: a denunciation of global inequality and cultural lobotomy, and scorn for social-democratic reformism, recalling his revolutionary past. But the

---

[39] 'Mur, golfe, système' (1990), in *Moralités Postmodernes*, pp. 67–68.

only resistances to the system that remained were inward: the reserve of the artist, the indeterminacy of childhood, the silence of the soul.[40] Gone was the 'jubilation' of the initial breakage of representation by the postmodern; an invincible malaise now defined the tone of the time. The postmodern was 'melancholy'.[41]

Frankfurt – Munich

The Postmodern Condition was published in the autumn of 1979. Exactly a year later, Jürgen Habermas delivered his address *Modernity – an Incomplete Project* in Frankfurt, on the occasion of his award of the Adorno prize by the city fathers. The lecture occupies a peculiar place in the discourse of postmodernity. Its substance touches only to a limited degree on the postmodern; yet the effect was to highlight it as a henceforth standard referent. This paradoxical outcome was largely, of course, due to Habermas's standing in the Anglo-Saxon world as premier European philosopher of the age. But it was also a function of the critical stance of his intervention. For the first time since the take-off of the idea of postmodernity in the late seventies, it received abrasive treatment. If the emergence of an intellectual terrain typically requires a negative pole for its productive tension, it was Habermas who supplied it.

---

[40] See, in particular, 'A l'insu' (1988), 'Ligne générale' (1991), and 'Intime est la terreur' (1993), in *Moralités Postmodernes*; and 'Avant-propos: de l'humain' (1988), in *L'Inhumain*, where Lyotard confesses: 'The inhumanity of the system now in the process of consolidation, under the name of development (among others), must not be confused with that, infinitely secret, of which the soul is hostage. To believe, as I once did, that the first kind of inhumanity can relay the second, give it expression, is an error. The effect of the system is rather to consign what escapes it to oblivion': p. 10. More recently, in 'La Mainmise', Lyotard reiterates the 'fable of development', but changes register: here it 'anticipates a contradiction' – for 'the process of development runs counter to the human design of emancipation', although it claims to be at one with it. To the question – 'Is there any instance within us that asks to be emancipated from this supposed emancipation?' – Lyotard's answer is the 'residue' bequeathed by 'immemorial childhood' to the 'gesture of witness' in the work of art: *Un Trait d'Union*, Paris 1993, p. 9.
[41] *Moralités Postmodernes*, pp. 93–94.

However, a misunderstanding has traditionally been attached to his text. Widely read as a response to Lyotard's work, because of the proximity of dates, in fact it was probably written in ignorance of the latter. Habermas was reacting rather to the Venice Biennale exhibition of 1980, the show-case for Jencks's version of postmodernism[42] – just what Lyotard, for his part, had been unaware of when producing his own. An ironic *chasse-croisé* of ideas stood at the origin of these exchanges.

Habermas began by acknowledging that the spirit of aesthetic modernity, with its new sense of time as a present charged with a heroic future, born in the epoch of Baudelaire and reaching a climax in Dada, had visibly waned; the avant-gardes had aged. The idea of postmodernity owed its power to this incontestable change. From it, however, neo-conservative theorists like Daniel Bell had drawn a perverse conclusion. The antinomian logic of modernist culture, they argued, had come to permeate the texture of capitalist society, weakening its moral fibre and undermining its work discipline with a cult of unrestrained subjectivity, at the very moment that this culture had ceased to be a source of creative art. The result threatened to be a hedonistic melt-down of a once honourable social order, that could only be checked by a revival of religious faith – in a world profaned, a return of the sacred.

This, Habermas observed, was to blame aesthetic modernism for what was all too obviously the commercial logic of capitalist modernization itself. The real aporias of cultural modernity lay elsewhere. The Enlightenment project of modernity had two strands. One was the differentiation for the first time of science, morality and art – no longer fused in a revealed religion – into autonomous value-spheres, each governed by its own norms – truth, justice, beauty. The other was the release of the potential

---

[42] 'Die Moderne – ein unvollendetes Projekt', *Kleine politische Schriften (I–IV)*, Frankfurt 1981, p. 444. This German address was significantly longer and sharper in tone than the English version delivered by Habermas as a James Lecture in New York the following year, published in *New German Critique*, Winter 1981, pp. 3–15. Its opening remarks ask the blunt question: 'Is the modern as out-dated as the postmoderns would have it? Or is the postmodern itself, proclaimed from so many sides, merely phony [sic]?'.

of these newly liberated domains into the subjective flux of daily life, interacting to enrich it. This was the programme that had gone astray. For instead of entering into the common resources of everyday communication, each sphere had tended to develop into an esoteric specialism, closed to the world of ordinary meanings. In the course of the nineteenth century art became a critical enclave increasingly alienated from society, even fetishizing its own distance from it. In the early twentieth century, revolutionary avant-gardes like surrealism had attempted to demolish the resultant division between art and life by spectacular acts of aesthetic will. But their gestures were futile: no emancipation flowed from destruction of forms or desublimation of meanings – nor could life have ever been transfigured by the absorption of art alone. That required a concurrent recovery of the resources of science and morality too, and the interplay of all three to animate the life-world.

The project of modernity had yet to be realized. But the outright attempt to negate it – a counsel of despair – had failed. The autonomy of the value-spheres could not be rescinded, on pain of regression. The need was still to reappropriate the expert cultures each had produced into the language of common experience. For this, however, there must be barriers to protect the spontaneity of the life-world from the incursions of market forces and of bureaucratic administration. But, Habermas gloomily conceded, 'the chances for this today are not very good. More or less everywhere in the entire Western world a climate has developed that furthers currents critical of cultural modernism'.[43] No less than three distinct brands of conservatism were now on offer. The anti-modernism of 'young' conservatives appealed to archaic, dionysiac powers against all

---

[43] To his German listeners, Habermas explained that a condition of 'a differentiated recoupling of modern culture with everyday praxis' was not just 'the ability of the life-world to develop institutions capable of limiting the internal dynamics of the economic and administrative action-systems' but *also the guiding of social modernization along other, non-capitalist paths*' – 'wenn *auch* die gesellschaftliche Modernisierung in *andere* nichtkapitalistische Bahnen gelenkt wurden kann'. Speaking to his American audience, Habermas discreetly dropped this clause, leaving only its anodyne pendant. Compare 'Die Moderne – ein unvollendetes Projekt', p. 462 with 'Modernity – an Incomplete Project', p. 13.

rationalization, in a tradition running from Bataille to Foucault. The pre-modernism of 'old' conservatives called for a substantive cosmological ethics of quasi-aristotelian stamp, along lines intimated by Leo Strauss. The postmodernism of 'neo-conservatives' welcomed the reification of separate value-spheres into closed domains of expertise armoured against any demands of the life-world, with conceptions of science close to those of the early Wittgenstein, of politics borrowed from Carl Schmitt, of art akin to those of Gottfried Benn. In Germany, a lurking blend of anti- and pre-modernism haunted the counter-culture, while an ominous alliance of pre- and post-modernism was taking shape in the political establishment.

Habermas's argument, compact in form, was nevertheless a curious construction. His definition of modernity, uncritically adopted from Weber, essentially reduced it to mere formal differentiation of value-spheres – to which he then subjoined, as an Enlightenment aspiration, their reconfiguration as inter-communicating resources in the life-world, an idea foreign to Weber and hard to detect in the *Aufklärung* (as distinct from Hegel) itself. What is clear enough, however, is that the 'project' of modernity as he sketched it is a contradictory amalgam of two opposite principles: specialization and popularization. How was a synthesis of the two at any stage to be realized? So defined, could the project ever be completed? But if in this sense it looks less unfinished than unfeasible, the reason lies in Habermas's social theory as a whole.

For the tensions of aesthetic modernity reproduce in minia-ture the strains in the structure of his account of capitalist societies at large. On the one hand, these are governed by 'systems' of impersonal coordination, mediated by the steering mechanisms of money and power, which cannot be recovered by any collective agency, on pain of regressive de-differentiation of separate institutional orders – market, administration, law, etc. On the other hand, the 'life-world' that is integrated by inter-subjective norms, in which communicative rather than instrumental action prevails, needs to be protected from 'colo-nization' by the systems – without, however, encroaching on them. What this dualism rules out is any form of pop-ular sovereignty, in either a traditional or radical sense. The self-government of freely associated producers is off the agenda. What is left is the velleity of an impossible reconciliation of two unequal domains. For the Habermas of *The Theory of Communicative Action* the 'public sphere' would be the democratic site of an annealing between the two – yet one whose structural decline he traced long ago. In *Modernity – an Incomplete Project*, there is no mention of it. But it has its echo in his single positive example of what a reappropriation of art in everyday existence might look like: the portrayal of young workers in pre-war Berlin discussing the Pergamon altar in Peter Weiss's *Aesthetics of Resistance*, reminiscent of the 'plebeian' equivalents of the bourgeois public sphere evoked in the preface to his famous study of the latter. But, of course, this is not only a fictive illustration. The aesthetic released is of classical antiquity, not modernity; set in a time, at that, before the avant-gardes had aged.

The *mal à propos* can be taken as an index of the underlying slippage in Habermas's argument. There is a basic disjuncture between the phenomenon it starts by registering – the apparent decline of aesthetic modernism – and the theme it goes on to develop – the overspecialization of value-spheres. The dynamic of science has clearly not been affected by the latter. Why should art be? Habermas attempts no answer: in fact, does not even pose the question. The result is a yawning gap between problem and solution. The waning of experimental vitality lies at one end of the address, the reanimation of the life-world at the other, and there is virtually no reasoned connexion between them. The misconstruction has its displaced symptom in the fanciful taxonomy with which it ends. Whatever the criticisms to be made of the intellectual descent from Bataille to Foucault (there are many), it cannot by any stretch of the imagination be described as 'conservative'. Vice-versa, however neo-conservative the progeny of Wittgenstein, Schmitt or Benn, not to speak of thinkers like Bell, to castigate them as vehicles of 'postmodernism' is peculiarly aberrant: they have typically been among its fiercest critics. To affix the label to such foes was tantamount to obnubilating the postmodern altogether.

This was not to be Habermas's last word on the subject, however. Less noticed, but more substantial was the lecture he

architecture

CRYSTALLIZATION

delivered on 'Modern and Postmodern Architecture' in Munich
a year later. Here Habermas engaged with the real stronghold
of postmodern aesthetic theory, displaying an impressive knowledge and passion about his subject. He started by observing that
the modern movement in architecture – the only unifying style
since neo-classicism – sprang from the spirit of the avant-garde,
yet had succeeded in creating a classic tradition true to the
inspiration of occidental rationalism. Today, it was under
widespread attack for the monstrous urban blight of so many
post-war cities. But 'is the real face of modern architecture
revealed in these atrocities, or are they distortions of its true
spirit'?[44] To answer this question, it was necessary to look back
at the origins of the movement.

In the nineteenth century, the industrial revolution had posed
three unprecedented challenges to the art of architecture. It
required the design of new kinds of buildings – both cultural
(libraries, schools, opera-houses) and economic (railway-
stations, department stores, warehouses, workers' housing); it
afforded new techniques and materials (iron, steel, concrete,
glass); and it imposed new social imperatives (market pressures,
administrative plans), in a 'capitalist mobilization of all urban
living conditions'.[45] These demands overwhelmed the architecture of the time, which failed to produce any coherent response
to them, disintegrating instead into eclectic historicism or grim
utility. Reacting to this failure in the early twentieth century,
the modern movement overcame the stylistic chaos and facti-
tious symbolism of late Victorian architecture, and set out to
transform the totality of the built environment, from the most
monumental and expressive edifices to the smallest and most
practical.

In doing so, it met the first two challenges of the industrial
revolution triumphantly, with extraordinary formal creativity.
But it was never able to master the third. Architectural modernism, virtually from the start, vastly overestimated its ability to

---

[44] 'Moderne und postmoderne Architektur', collected in *Die Neue Unübersicht-
lichkeit*, Frankfurt 1985, p. 15; English translation in *The New Conservatism*,
Cambridge, Mass. 1989, p. 8.
[45] 'Moderne und postmoderne Architektur', p. 18.

41

re-shape the urban environment: a miscalculation famously expressed in the hubris of the early, utopian Le Corbusier. After the war, this strain of naiveté rendered it helpless before the pressures of capitalist reconstruction, that led to the desolate cityscapes for which it later had to shoulder the blame. At the end of this itinerary, lay the backlash of the present scene: a conservative reversion to neo-historicism (Terry), a vitalist quest for community architecture (Kier), and the flamboyant stage-sets of postmodernism proper (Hollein or Venturi). In all, the unity of form and function that had driven the project of modernism was now dissolved.

This was certainly a more telling account of the fate of aesthetic modernity, in the most socially sensitive of all the arts, than the Frankfurt lecture. But the Munich address, though much richer and more precise, still posed the same underlying problem. What had ultimately caused the downfall in public esteem of the modern movement in architecture? On the surface, the answer was clear: its inability to resist or outflank the constraints of post-war money and power: 'the contradictions of capitalist modernization', as Habermas at one point puts it.[46] But how far was architectural modernism – wittingly or unwittingly – complicit with these imperatives? Habermas accords it some responsibility, for misunderstanding its own original dynamic. Historically, the roots of modernism lay in three responses to cubism in the field of pure design: Russian constructivism, De Stijl, and the circle around Le Corbusier. Experimental form engendered practical function, rather than the other way round. But as the Bauhaus acquired dominance, it forgot its origins and misrepresented the new architecture as 'functionalist'. In the end, this confusion lent itself all too readily to exploitation by developers and bureaucrats, commissioning and financing buildings that were functional to them.

But this unseeing betrayal of itself, however serious, was not the efficient cause of the impasse of modernism. That lay in the insuperable constraints of its social environment. At first glance, Habermas here appeared to be indicting the ruthless speculative logic of post-war capitalism, scattering brutal office blocks and

[46] Ibid., p. 23.

42

jerry-built high-rises across the urban landscape. If this were so, then a radical social reversal could be imagined, in which the dictates of profit were swept away and the urban fabric healed by the collective enabling of an architecture of shelter, sociability, beauty. This, however, is just what Habermas effectively rules out. For the ultimate error of modernism, he explains, was not so much lack of vigilance towards the market, as too much trust in the plan. Not the commands of capital, but necessities of modernity – the structural differentiation of society, rather than the pursuit of rent or profit – condemned it to frustration. 'The utopia of preconceived forms of life that had already inspired the designs of Owen and Fourier could not be realized, not only because of a hopeless underestimation of the diversity, complexity and variability of modern societies, but also because modernized societies with their functional interdependencies go beyond the dimensions of living conditions that could be gauged by the imagination of the planner'.[47]

Here, in other words, recurs the schema traced by the Frankfurt address, derived from the same paralysed dualism set up by Habermas's theory of communication action: inviolable systems and inoperative life-worlds. But there at least the possibility of some recovery of leeway by the latter is nominally kept open. Here, Habermas draws the consequences from his premises more implacably. It was not just modernist dreams of a humane city that were impracticable. The very idea of a city at all is condemned to obsolescence by the functional exigencies of impersonal coordination, that render any attempt to recreate coherent urban meaning futile. Once, 'the city could be architecturally designed and mentally represented as a comprehensible habitat'. But with industrialism the city became 'embedded in abstract systems which could no longer be captured aesthetically in an intelligible presence'.[48]

From the beginning, proletarian housing could never be integrated into the metropolis; and as time went on, proliferating sub-zones of commercial or administrative activity dispersed it yet further into an ungraspable, featureless maze. 'The graphics

[47] Ibid., p. 23.
[48] Ibid., p. 25.

43

of company trade-marks and neon advertisements demonstrate that differentiation must take place by means other than the formal language of architecture'. There is no turning back from this fate. 'Urban agglomerations have outgrown the old concept of the city we still keep in our hearts. However, that is neither the failure of modern architecture, nor of any other architecture'.[49] It is written into the logic of social development, beyond capital or labour, as a requirement of modernity itself. Not financial accumulation but systemic coordination, that cannot be cancelled, renders urban space indecipherable.

Here the pathos of Habermas's later theory, which simultaneously reaffirms the ideals of the Enlightenment and denies them any chance of realization, finds its purest expression: what might be called, inverting Gramsci's formula, eudaemonism of the intelligence, defeatism of the will. Habermas ends by expressing a guarded sympathy for vernacular currents in architecture that encourage popular participation in design projects, as a trend wherein some of the impulses of the Modern Movement defensively survive. But – just as in the wider counter-culture – 'nostalgia for de-differentiated forms of existence bestows on these tendencies an air of anti-modernism'[50]: their tacit appeal to a *Volksgeist* recalls the dire example, however distinct in monumental intention, of Nazi architecture. If Habermas concedes, without enthusiasm, that there is a good deal of 'truth' in this form of opposition, what he does not – cannot – say is that there is any hope in it.

There, in the autumn of 1981, matters stood. Thirty years after a sense of it was first aired by Olson, the postmodern had crystallized as common referent and competing discourse. In its origins, the idea was always brushed by associations beyond the West – China, Mexico, Turkey; even later, behind Hassan or Lyotard lay Egypt and Algeria, and the anomaly of Quebec. Space was inscribed in it from the start. Culturally, it pointed beyond what had become of modernism; but in what direction, there was no consensus, only a set of oppositions going back to

[49] Ibid., p. 26.
[50] Ibid., p. 27.

De Onís; and in what arts or sciences, only disconnected interests and criss-crossing opinions. The coincident interventions of Lyotard and Habermas for the first time sealed the field with the stamp of philosophical authority. But their own contributions were each strangely indecisive. The original background of both thinkers was Marxist, but it is striking how little of it they brought to their accounts of postmodernity. Neither attempted any real historical interpretation of the postmodern, capable of determining it in time or space. Instead, they offered more or less floating or vacant signifiers as the mark of its appearance: the delegitimation of grand narratives (dateless) for Lyotard, the colonization of the life-world (when was it not colonized?) for Habermas. Paradoxically, a concept by definition temporal lacks periodic weight in either.

Nor is the haze that envelops the term as social development dispelled by its usage as aesthetic category. Both Lyotard and Habermas were deeply attached to the principles of high modernism; but far from this commitment enabling them to bring postmodernism into sharper focus, it seems to have occluded it. Recoiling from unwelcome evidence of what it might mean, Lyotard was reduced to denying that it was other than an inner fold of the modernism itself. Habermas, more willing to engage with the arts in view, could acknowledge a passage from the modern to the postmodern, but was scarcely able to explain it. Neither ventured any exploration of postmodern forms to compare with the detailed discussions of Hassan or Jencks. The net effect was a discursive dispersion: on the one hand, philosophical overview without significant aesthetic content, on the other aesthetic insight without coherent theoretical horizon. A thematic crystallization had occurred – the postmodern was now, as Habermas put it, 'on the agenda' – without intellectual integration.

The field, however, did display another kind of unity: it was ideologically consistent. The idea of the postmodern, as it took hold in this conjuncture, was in one way or another an appanage of the Right. Hassan, lauding play and indeterminacy as hallmarks of the postmodern, made no secret of his aversion to the sensibility that was their antithesis: the iron yoke of the Left. Jencks celebrated the passing of the modern as the liberation of consumer choice, a quietus to planning in a world where painters could trade as freely and globally as bankers. For Lyotard the very parameters of the new condition were set by the discrediting of socialism as the last grand narrative – ultimate version of an emancipation that no longer held meaning. Habermas, resisting allegiance to the postmodern, from a position still on the Left, nevertheless conceded the idea to the Right, construing it as a figure of neo-conservatism. Common to all was subscription to the principles of what Lyotard – once the most radical – called liberal democracy, as the unsurpassable horizon of the time. There could be nothing but capitalism. The postmodern was a sentence on alternative illusions.

===================== 3 =====================

Capture

Such was the situation when Fredric Jameson gave his first [7] lecture on postmodernism in the fall of 1982. Two works had established him as the world's leading Marxist literary critic, although he had already made the terms too restrictive. *Marxism and Form* (1971) was an original reconstruction, through studies of Lukács, Bloch, Adorno, Benjamin and Sartre, of virtually the complete intellectual canon of Western Marxism between *History and Class Consciousness* and the *Critique of Dialectical Reason*, from the standpoint of a contemporary aesthetics true to its many-sided legacy. *The Prison-House of Language* (1972) offered a complementary account of the linguistic model developed by Saussure and its projections in Russian formalism and French structuralism, concluding with the semiotics of Barthes and Greimas: an admiring but stringent survey of the merits and limits of a synchronic tradition that set its face against the temptations of temporality.

Sources

Jameson's own commitments as a critic were firm and distinctive. They are perhaps best captured by his Afterword to *Aesthetics and Politics* (1976), a volume collecting the classic debates that had ranged Lukács, Brecht, Bloch, Benjamin and Adorno against each other. For Jameson, writing just as notions of postmodernism were beginning to circulate in literature departments, what was at stake in these exchanges was 'the aesthetic conflict between realism and modernism, whose navigation and renegotiation is still unavoidable for us today'.[1] If each retained its truth, yet neither could any longer be accepted as such, the emphasis of Jameson's account fell, subtly but umistakeably, on the unregarded side of the opposition. While noting the deficiencies of Lukács's attempt to prolong traditional forms of realism into the present, he pointed out that Brecht could not be taken simply as a modernist antidote, given his own hostility to purely formal experimentation. Brecht and Benjamin had indeed looked towards a revolutionary art capable of appropriating modern technology to reach popular audiences – while Adorno had more speciously contended that the formal logic of high modernism itself, in its very autonomy and abstraction, was the only true refuge of politics. But the post-war development of consumer capitalism had struck away the possibility of either: the entertainments industry mocking the hopes of Brecht or Benjamin, while an establishment culture mummified the exempla of Adorno.

The result was a present in which 'both alternatives of realism and modernism seem intolerable to us: realism because its forms revive an older experience of a kind of life that is no longer with us in the already decayed future of consumer society; modernism because its contradictions have in practice proved more acute than those of realism'. Precisely here, it might be thought, lay an opening for postmodernism as the art of the age. What is striking in retrospect, however, is not so much that this resolution is avoided. It is considered and rejected. 'An aesthetic of novelty today – already enthroned as the dominant critical and formal ideology – must seek desperately to renew itself by ever more rapid rotations of its own axis, modernism seeking to become postmodernism without ceasing to be modern.' The signs of such involution were the return of figurative art, as a representation of images rather than things in photo-realism, and the revival of intrigue in fiction, with a pastiche of classical narratives. Jameson's conclusion was a calculated defiance of this logic, turning its terms against itself. 'In circumstances like

---

[1] 'Reflections in Conclusion' to Ernst Bloch et al., *Aesthetic and Politics*, London 1977, p. 196; reprinted as 'Reflections on the Brecht–Lukács Debate', in *The Ideologies of Theory*, Vol 1, Minneapolis 1988, p. 133.

these, there is some question whether the ultimate renewal of
modernism, the final dialectical subversion of the now automa-
tized conventions of an aesthetic of perpetual revolution, might
not simply be . . . realism itself!'. Since the estranging techniques
of modernism had degenerated into standardized conventions
of cultural consumption, it was their 'habit of fragmentation'
that now itself needed to be estranged in some freshly totalizing
art. The debates of the inter-war period thus had a paradoxical
lesson for the present. 'In an unexpected dénouement, it may be
Lukács – wrong as he might have been in the 1930s – who has
the provisional last word for us today'. The contradictory legacy
of those years leaves contemporaries with a precise but impon-
derable task. 'It cannot of course tell us what our conception of
realism ought to be; yet its study makes it impossible for us not
to feel the obligation to reinvent one'.[2]

Jameson's initial glimpse of postmodernism thus tended to
see it as the sign of a kind of inner deliquescence within
modernism, the remedy for which lay in a new realism, yet to
be imagined. The tensions within this position found further,
and still more pointed expression in the programmatic essay he
published on 'The Ideology of the Text' at virtually the same
time. For this critical intervention opens with the words: 'All
the straws in the wind seem to confirm the wide-spread feeling
that "modern times are now over" and that some fundamental
divide, some basic *coupure* or qualitative leap, now separates us
decisively from what used to be the new world of the early
twentieth century, of triumphant modernism'. Among the
phenomena that testified to 'some irrevocable distance from the
immediate past' – alongside the role of computers, of genetics,
of détente, and others – was 'postmodernism in literature and
art'. All such shifts, Jameson remarked, tended to generate
ideologies of change, usually apologetic in cast, where a theory
capable of connecting the current 'great transformation' to 'the
long-range destiny of our socio-economic system' was needed.[3]

[2] *Aesthetics and Politics*, pp. 211–213; *The Ideologies of Theory*, Vol 2, Minneapolis 1988, pp. 145–147.
[3] 'The Ideology of the Text', *Salmagundi*, No 31–32, Fall 1975–Winter 1976,
pp. 204–205; revised version, *The Ideologies of Theory*, Vol 1, pp. 17–18.

One such ideology, of particular interest and influence, was the current idea of textuality.

Taking Barthes's study of Balzac's novella *Sarrasine* as exemplary of the new style of literary analysis – Barthes himself as a 'fever-chart' of successive intellectual fashions – Jameson argued that it could be read as a kind of replay of the realism/modernism controversy. Transformed by Barthes into an opposition between the legible and the scriptible, the duality encouraged censorious judgements of realist narratives, whose moralism functioned as compensation for an inability to situate formal differences in a diachronic history, without ideological praise or blame. The best antidote to such evaluations was to 'historicize the binary opposition, by adding a third term'. For 'everything changes, the moment we envisage a "before" to realism itself' – mediaeval tales, renaissance novellas, which reveal the peculiar modernity of nineteenth century forms themselves, as a unique and unrepeatable vehicle of the cultural revolution needed to adapt human beings to the new conditions of industrial existence. In this sense, 'realism and modernism must be seen as specific and determinate historical expressions of the type of socio-economic structures to which they correspond, namely classical capitalism and consumer capitalism.' If this was not the place for a full Marxist account of that sequence, 'it certainly is the moment to square accounts with the *ideology* of modernism which has given its title to the present essay'.[4]

The significance of this passage was to lie in its revision. Jameson's supple and ingenious critique of Barthes nevertheless left a detectable lacuna between its initial premise and such a conclusion. For 'The Ideology of the Text' had started by registering a fundamental divide between the present and the time of modernism, now declared 'over'. If that intuition was right, how could one of the symptoms of this change, the idea of textuality, be little more than an ideology of what preceded it? It was this logical gap that, when he revised the essay for book publication twelve years later, Jameson moved to close. Here, retrospectively, can be located with great precision the

---

[4] 'The Ideology of the Text', *Salmagundi*, No 31–32, pp. 234, 242.

threshold to be crossed for a turn to the postmodern. Deleting the passage above, he now wrote: 'The attempt to unsettle this seemingly ineradicable dualism by adding a third term, in the form of some "classical" – or pre-capitalist – narrative proved to have only partial success, modifying Barthes's working categories but not his fundamental historical scheme. Let us therefore attempt to displace this last in a different way, by introducing a third term as it were at the other end of its temporal spectrum. The concept of *postmodernism* in fact incorporates all the features of the Barthesian aesthetic'.[5]

This was the view that, tantalizingly close, still remained just out of reach in the late seventies. Other texts of the period hesitate at the same ford. What enabled Jameson to make the passage with such *brio* at the Whitney – delivering a complete theory, virtually at a stroke – a few years later? Some of the sources of the change in direction were later to be noted by Jameson himself; others remain a matter for conjecture. The first and most important lay in his own initial sense of the novelty of post-war capitalism. The very first pages of *Marxism and Form* stressed the sundering of all continuity with the past by the new modes of organization of capital. 'The reality with which the Marxist criticism of the 1930's had to deal was that of a simpler Europe and America, which no longer exist. Such a world had more in common with the life-forms of earlier centuries than it does with our own'. The receding of class conflict within the metropolis, while violence was projected without; the enormous weight of advertising and media fantasy in suppressing the realities of division and exploitation; the disconnexion of private and public existence – all this had created a society without precedent. 'In psychological terms, we may say that as a service economy we are henceforth so far removed from the realities of production and work that we inhabit a dream world of artificial stimuli and televised experience: never in any previous civilization have the great metaphysical preoccupations, the fundamental questions of being and of the meaning of life, seemed so utterly remote and pointless'.[6]

[5] *The Ideologies of Theory*, Vol 1, p. 66. Written in the late eighties.
[6] *Marxism and Form*, Princeton 1971, pp. xvii–xviii.

Here, right from the start, can be seen the origins of themes that were to figure so largely in Jameson's later work on postmodernism. Two influences, by his own account, helped to develop them, enabling him to stage each to quite new effect in the eighties. One was the publication of Ernest Mandel's *Late Capitalism*, which offered the first systematic theory of the history of capital to appear since the war, providing the basis – empirical and conceptual – for understanding the present as a qualitatively new configuration in the trajectory of this mode of production. Jameson was to express his debt to this path-breaking work on many occasions. A second – lesser, though still significant – stimulus came from Baudrillard's writing on the role of the simulacrum in the cultural imaginary of contemporary capitalism.[7] This was a line of thinking Jameson had anticipated, but Baudrillard's time in San Diego when Jameson was teaching there certainly had an impact on him. The difference, of course, is that by this date Baudrillard – originally close to the Situationists – vehemently dismissed the Marxist legacy that Mandel set out to develop.

Another kind of catalyst can probably be traced to Jameson's departure for Yale at the end of the seventies. For this, of course, was the university whose Art and Architecture building, designed by Paul Rudolph, doubling as dean of the school of architecture, had been singled out by Venturi as an epitome of the null brutalism into which the Modern Movement had declined, and where Venturi, Scully and Moore all taught themselves. Jameson thus found himself in the vortex of architectural conflicts between the modern and the postmodern. In good-humouredly recording that this was the art that awakened

---

[7] For Jameson's acknowledgement of these sources, see 'Marxism and Postmodernism', in *The Cultural Turn – Selected Writings on the Postmodern, 1983–1998*, London–New York 1998, pp. 34–35. Baudrillard presents a special case for any genealogy of the postmodern. For although his ideas certainly contributed to its crystallization, and his style can be regarded as paradigmatic of its form, he himself has never theorized postmodernism, and his single extended pronouncement on it is a virulent repudiation: see 'The Anorexic Ruins', in D. Kamper and C. Wulf (eds), *Looking Back at the End of the World*, New York 1989, pp. 41–42. This is a thinker whose temper, for better or worse, is incapable of assent to any notion with collective acceptance.

him from 'dogmatic slumbers', Jameson no doubt refers to this setting. It might be better to say that it released him for the visual. Up to the eighties, Jameson had concentrated his attention all but exclusively on literature. The turn to a theory of the postmodern was, at the same stroke, to be an arresting shift to the range of arts – nearly the full range – beyond it. This involved no drift of political moorings. In the immediate case of the built environment, he had a significant resource to hand within the legacy of Western Marxism in the work of Henri Lefebvre – another guest in California. Jameson was perhaps the first outside France to make good use of Lefebvre's corpus of suggestive ideas on the urban and spatial dimensions of postwar capitalism; as he was later quick to register the formidable architectural writing of the Venetian critic Manfredo Tafuri, a Marxist of more Adornian stamp.

Finally there was perhaps the direct provocation posed by Lyotard himself. When an English translation of *La Condition Postmoderne* was at length ready in 1982, Jameson was asked to write an introduction to it. Lyotard's assault on meta-narratives might have been aimed specifically at him. For just a year before he had published a major work of literary theory, *The Political Unconscious*, whose central argument was the most eloquent and express claim for Marxism *as* a grand narrative ever made. 'Only Marxism can give us an adequate sense of the essential *mystery* of the cultural past', he wrote – a 'mystery [that] can only be reenacted if the human adventure is one'. Only thus could such long-dead issues as a tribal transhumance, a theological controversy, clashes in the *polis*, duels in nineteenth century parliaments, come alive again. 'These matters can recover their urgency for us only if they are retold within the unity of a single great collective story; only if, in however disguised and symbolic a form, they are seen as sharing a single fundamental theme – for Marxism, the collective struggle to wrest a realm of Freedom from a realm of Necessity; only if they are grasped as vital episodes in a single vast unfinished plot'.[8] When Lyotard launched his attack, no Marxist had ever actually presented Marxism as in essence a narrative

---

[8] *The Political Unconscious*, Ithaca 1981, pp. 19–20.

– it was more commonly understood as an analytic. But two years later, as if on demand, Jameson offered exactly what Lyotard had supposed.

But if in this sense *The Postmodern Condition* must, when he came upon it, have been the most direct challenge to Jameson conceivable, another side of Lyotard's argument was uncannily similar to his own. For the premise of both thinkers – spelt out, if anything, even more emphatically by Lyotard than Jameson – was that narrative was a fundamental instance of the human mind.[9] The provocation of Lyotard's account of postmodernity must thus to some extent also have acted as an ambivalent foil for Jameson, quickening his own reflections on the subject. The difficult task of introducing a work with whose overall stance he can have had so little sympathy, he acquitted with grace and guile. Lyotard's case was certainly striking. But in its concentration on the sciences, it said little about developments in culture, and was not very forthcoming about politics, or their ground in changes in socio-economic life.[10] Here was the agenda to which Jameson would now turn.

Five Moves

The founding text which opens *The Cultural Turn*, Jameson's lecture to the Whitney Museum of Contemporary Arts in the fall of 1982, which became the nucleus of his essay 'Postmodernism – the Cultural Logic of Late Capitalism' published in *New Left Review* in the spring of 1984, redrew the whole map of the postmodern at one stroke – a prodigious inaugural gesture that has commanded the field ever since. Five decisive moves marked this intervention. The first, and most fundamental, came with its title – the anchorage of postmodernism in objective alterations of the economic order of capital itself. No

[9] For Lyotard, not only was 'narration the quintessential form of customary knowledge' before the arrival of modern science, but 'the little narrative remains the quintessential form of imaginative invention, most particularly in science': *La Condition Postmoderne*, pp. 38 and 98; *The Postmodern Condition*, pp. 19 and 60; while Jameson viewed 'story-telling as the supreme function of the human mind': *The Political Unconscious*, p. 123.

[10] 'Foreword' to *The Postmodern Condition*, pp. xii–xv.

longer mere aesthetic break or epistemological shift, postmodernity becomes the cultural signal of a new stage in the history of the regnant mode of production. It is striking that this idea, before which Hassan had hesitated and then turned away, was quite foreign to Lyotard and Habermas, although both came from Marxist backgrounds by no means altogether extinct.

At the Whitney, the term 'consumer society' acted as a kind of preliminary range-finder for a survey at higher resolution to come. In the subsequent version, for *New Left Review*, the 'new moment of multi-national capitalism' came more fully into focus. Here Jameson pointed to the technological explosion of modern electronics, and its role as leading edge of profit and innovation; to the organizational predominance of transnational corporations, outsourcing manufacturing operations to cheap-wage locations overseas; to the immense increase in the range of international speculation; and to the rise of media conglomerates wielding unprecedented power across communications and borders alike. These developments had profound consequences for every dimension of life in advanced industrial countries – business cycles, employment patterns, class relationships, regional fates, political axes. But in a longer view, the most fundamental change of all lay in the new existential horizon of these societies. Modernization was now all but complete, obliterating the last vestiges not only of pre-capitalist social forms, but every intact natural hinterland, of space or experience, that had sustained or survived them.

In a universe thus abluted of nature, culture has necessarily expanded to the point where it has become virtually coextensive with the economy itself, not merely as the symptomatic basis of some of the largest industries in the world – tourism now exceeding all other branches of global employment – but much more deeply, as every material object and immaterial service becomes inseparably tractable sign and vendible commodity. Culture in this sense, as the inescapable tissue of life under late capitalism, is now our second nature. Where modernism drew its purpose and energies from the persistence of what was not yet modern, the legacy of a still pre-industrial past, postmodernism signifies the closure of that distance, the saturation of every pore of the world in the serum of capital. Marked out by no stark political caesura, no sudden storm in the historical heavens, this 'very modest or mild apocalypse, the merest sea-breeze'[11] represents a momentous transformation in the underlying structures of contemporary bourgeois society.

What have been the consequences of this change in the object-world for the experience of the subject? Jameson's second distinctive move was an exploration of the metastases of the psyche in this new conjuncture. Initially broached as terse commentary on the 'death of the subject', his development of this theme soon became perhaps the most famous of all facets of his construction of the postmodern. In a series of arresting phenomenological descriptions, Jameson sketched the *Lebenswelt* characteristic of the time, as the spontaneous forms of the postmodern sensibility. This was a psychic landscape, he argued, whose ground had been broken by the great turmoil of the sixties – when so many traditional casings of identity were broken apart by the dissolution of customary constraints – but now, after the political defeats of the seventies, purged of all radical residues. Among the traits of the new subjectivity, in fact, was the loss of any active sense of history, either as hope or memory. The charged sense of the past – as either ague-bed of repressive traditions, or reservoir of thwarted dreams; and heightened expectancy of the future – as potential cataclysm or transfiguration – which had characterized modernism, was gone. At best, fading back into a perpetual present, retro-styles and images proliferated as surrogates of the temporal.

In the age of the satellite and optical fibre, on the other hand, the spatial commands this imaginary as never before. The electronic unification of the earth, instituting the simultaneity of events across the globe as daily spectacle, has lodged a vicarious geography in the recesses of every consciousness, while the encircling networks of multinational capital that actually direct the system exceed the capacities of any perception. The ascendency of space over time in the make-up of the postmodern is thus always off-balance: the realities to which it answers constitutively overpowering it – inducing, Jameson suggests in a celebrated passage, that sensation which is only to be captured

---

[11] *Postmodernism, or, the Cultural Logic of Late Capitalism*, Durham 1991, p. xiv.

by a sardonic updating of the lesson of Kant: the 'hysterical sublime'.

Conventionally hysteria denotes an overpitching of emotion, a half-conscious feigning of intensity the better to conceal some inner numbness (or psychoanalytically, the other way round). For Jameson, this is a general condition of postmodern experience, marked by a 'waning of affect' that ensues as the bounded self of old begins to fray. The result is a new depthlessness of the subject, no longer held within stable parameters, where the registers of high and low are unequivocal. Here, by contrast, psychic life becomes unnervingly accidented and spasmodic, marked by sudden dips of level or lurches of mood, that recall something of the fragmentation of schizophrenia. This swerving, stammering flux precludes either cathexis or historicity. Significantly, to the vacillations of libidinal investment in private life has corresponded an erosion of generational markers in public memory, as the decades since the sixties have tended to flatten out into a featureless sequence subsumed under the common roster of the postmodern itself. But if such discontinuity weakens the sense of difference between periods at the social level, its effects are far from monotone at the individual level. There, on the contrary, the typical polarities of the subject run from the elation of the 'commodity rush', the euphoric highs of spectator or consumer, to the dejection at the bottom of 'the deeper nihilistic void of our being', as prisoners of an order that resists any other control or meaning.[12]

Having set out the force-field of postmodernity in structural changes of late capitalism, and a pervasive laddering of identities under them, Jameson could make his third move, on the terrain of culture itself. Here his innovation was topical. Hitherto, every sounding of the postmodern had been sectoral. Levin and Fiedler had detected it in literature; Hassan enlarged it to painting and music, if more by allusion than by exploration; Jencks concentrated on architecture; Lyotard dwelt on science; Habermas touched on philosophy. Jameson's work has been of another scope – a majestic expansion of the postmodern across virtually the whole spectrum of the arts, and much of the

[12] *Postmodernism*, pp. 317.

discourse flanking them. The result is an incomparably richer and more comprehensive mural of the age than any other record of this culture.

Architecture, the spur to Jameson's turn beyond the modern, has always remained at the centre of his vision of what succeeded it. His first extended analysis of a postmodern work was the great set-piece on Portman's *Bonaventure* hotel in Los Angeles, whose début is to be found below – on the evidence of citation, the most memorable single exercise in all the literature on postmodernism. Jameson's later meditations have picked a deliberate path through a crowded field of candidates for commentary: first Gehry, then Eisenmann and Koolhaas. The paramountcy of space in the categorical framework of postmodern understanding, as he read it, more or less ensured that architecture would have pride of place in the cultural mutation of late capitalism at large. Here, Jameson has consistently argued, explosive energies of invention have been released, in a range of forms from the spare to the sumptuous, that no rival art today can match; while at the same time also figuring, more graphically than any other art, different kinds of subsumption to the new world economic system, or attempts to elude it – not only in the practical dependence of its airports, hotels, bourses, museums, villas or ministries on estimates of profit or whims of prestige, but in the tangibility of its shapes themselves.

Next in the system of postmodern arts comes the cinema. Surprising though it may seem in retrospect, film was a conspicuous absence in earlier discussion of postmodernism. Not that this silence was quite inexplicable. The principal reason for it can probably be found in a famous remark of Michael Fried: 'the cinema is not, even at its most experimental, a modernist art'.[13] He meant in part that film, as the most mixed of all mediums, was debarred from that drive to a purity of presence specific to each art, absolved of reference to any other, that Greenberg had held to be the royal road of the modern. But the judgement could be taken in another, more widely felt sense. For had not the triumph of Hollywood realism actually reversed

[13] 'Art and Objecthood', *Artforum*, June 1967; reprinted in G. Battcock (ed), *Minimal Art*, Berkeley and Los Angeles, 1995, p. 141.

film/video

the trajectory of modernism, Technicolor banishing the audacities of silent cinema to the pre-history of the industry? Such, at any rate, was the challenge that Jameson came to take up.

His initial interest was caught by a filmic genre that he eventually dubbed with a suggestive oxymoron 'nostalgia for the present': films like *Body Heat* or in another key *Star Wars*, or yet again *Blue Velvet*, that express even more deeply than the wave of *mode rétro* movies proper – over two decades of output now, from *American Graffiti* to *Indochine* – the peculiarly postmodern loss of any sense of the past, in a hidden contamination of the actual by the wistful, a time yearning for itself at an impotent, covert remove. If such forms, surrogates or displacements of true periodic memory, trace a corruption of the temporal, other genres can be read as responses to the arrival of the ultra-spatial: above all, the conspiracy film – *Videodrome* or *The Parallax View*, interpreted as blind allegories of the unrepresentable totality of global capital and its impersonal networks of power.

In due course, Jameson proceeded to the fuller theorization of the history of the cinema which lay in the logic of his enquiry. There were two separate cycles in the development of this art, he argued. Silent film had indeed followed a path from realism to modernism, if one – by reason of its timing as a technical possibility – out of rhythm with the move from national to imperial capitalism that otherwise presided over this transition. But this development was cut off by sound before there could be any chance of a postmodern moment. A second cycle then recapitulated the same phases at a new technological level, Hollywood inventing a screen realism with a panoply of narrative genres and visual conventions all its own, and the European art cinema of the post-war years producing a fresh wave of high modernism. If the postmodern cinema that had since appeared was stamped by the compulsions of nostalgia, the fortunes of the moving image in this period were by no means locked on them alone. Indeed, video was more likely to emerge as the peculiarly postmodern medium – whether in the dominant forms of commercial television, in which entertainment and advertising were now virtually fused, or in the oppositional practices of underground video. Inevitably, the criticism of the future would have to concern itself increasingly with these.

The world of graphic design and advertising, in turn, now increasingly interpenetrated with the fine arts, as impulse to style or source of material. In pictorial space, postmodern depthlessness had found perfected expression in the enervated surfaces of Warhol's work, with their hypnotically empty after-images of the fashion page, the supermarket shelf, the television screen. Here Jameson was to stage the most bravura of all juxtapositions between high modern and postmodern, in a comparison of Van Gogh's peasant boots, emblems of earthly labour redeemed in a pyre of colour, and one of Warhol's sets of pumps, vitreous simulacra without tone or ground, suspended in an icy void. The arrival of Pop Art had, in fact, long been noted by Jameson as a barometric warning of atmospheric changes under way – presages of a wider cultural anti-cyclone to come. Once fully in the postmodern, however, his attention moved to practices that sought to outrange the conventions this moment had left behind, in a conceptual art breaking free of the pictorial frame altogether. In the installations of Robert Gober, reveries of unplaceable community, and Hans Haacke, battle-kits of forensic insurgency, alternative kinds of imagination – owing something to Emerson or Adorno – wrest utopian clearances out of the claustral pressures of the postmodern itself.

Such radical energies, released as the boundaries between painting and sculpture, building and landscape increasingly dissolve, belong to a wider productivity, observable in many more pliable forms. Peculiar to this culture, Jameson remarks, is a privilege of the visual that marks it off from high modern-ism, in which the verbal still retained most of its ancient authority. Not that literature has been less affected by the change of period; but in Jameson's view less original work has been generated by it. For here, perhaps more than in any other art, the most insistent motif of the new was a – playful or portentous – parasitism on the old. In Jameson's texts, the name of this device is pastiche. The source of this usage lay in Adorno's critique of what he took to be the regressive eclecti-cism of Stravinsky in *The Philosophy of Modern Music*; but

Jameson gave it a more pointed definition. Pastiche was a 'blank parody', without satiric impulse, of the styles of the past. Spreading from architecture to film, painting to rock-music, it had become the most standardized signature of the postmodern, across every art. But it might be argued that fiction was now the domain of pastiche *par excellence*. For here mimicry of the defunct, unhampered by building codes or box office constraints, could shuffle not only styles but also periods themselves at will – revolving and splicing 'artificial' pasts, blending the documentary and fantastic, proliferating anachronisms, in a massive revival of – what must perforce still be termed – the historical novel. Jameson spotted this form at its inception, in an elegiac reading of Doctorow's political fictions of a radical American past, now forgotten, where the impossibility of holding steady any historical referent shadows the very eclipse the novels mourn.

Alongside these changes in the arts, and sometimes indeed directly at work within them, the discourses traditionally concerned with the cultural field have undergone an implosion of their own. What were once the sharply separate disciplines of art history, literary criticism, sociology, political science, history started to lose their clear edges, and cross with each in hybrid, transverse enquiries that could no longer easily be allotted to one or other domain. The work of Michel Foucault, Jameson noted, was a foremost example of such an unassignable oeuvre. What was replacing the old divisions of the disciplines was a new discursive phenomenon, best indicated by its American short-hand: 'Theory'. The distinctive form of much of this work reflected the increasing textualization of its objects – what could be called a revival, immensely more versatile, of the ancient practice of 'commentary'. Leading examples of this style in literary studies were the deconstructive writing of Paul DeMan, and the 'new historicism' of Walter Benn Michael, bodies of work Jameson has submitted to admiring but severe criticism, without rejecting the development itself – of which his own work on Adorno could in many ways be regarded as a remarkable example.

Beyond its immediate effects, what this reorganization of the intellectual field signalled was a more fundamental break. The hallmark of modernity, Weber had classically argued, was structural differentiation: the autonomization of practices and values, once closely mingled in social experience, into sharply separate domains. This is the process that Habermas has always insisted cannot be cancelled, on pain of retrogression. On such premises, there could be no more ominous symptom of some cracking in the modern than the break-down of these hard-won divisions. This was the process Fried had foreseen and feared in 1967. A decade later, it had not just spread from the arts into the humanities or social sciences, but with the arrival of the philosophical post-card and the conceptual neon-sign, was eroding the line between them. What postmodernity seemed to spell was something the great theorists of modernization had ruled out: an unthinkable de-differentiation of cultural spheres.

Anchorage of postmodernism in the transformations of capital; probing of the alterations of the subject; extension of the span of cultural enquiry – after these, Jameson could make a logical fourth move. What were the social bases and geopolitical pattern of postmodernism? Late capitalism remained a class society, but no class within it was quite the same as before. The immediate vector of postmodern culture was certainly to be found in the stratum of newly affluent employees and professionals created by the rapid growth of the service and speculative sectors of the developed capitalist societies. Above this brittle yuppie layer loomed the massive structures of multinational corporations themselves – vast servo-mechanisms of production and power, whose operations criss-cross the global economy, and determine its representations in the collective imaginary. Below, as an older industrial order is churned up, traditional class formations have weakened, while segmented identities and localized groups, typically based on ethnic or sexual differences, multiply. On a world scale – in the postmodern epoch, the decisive arena – no stable class structure, comparable to that of an earlier capitalism, has yet crystallized. Those above have the coherence of privilege; those below lack unity and solidarity. A new 'collective labourer' has yet to emerge. These are conditions, still, of a certain vertical indefinition.

At the same time, the sudden horizontal enlargement of the

system, with the integration for the first time of virtually the whole planet into the world market, means the entry of new peoples onto the global stage, whose human weight is rapidly increasing. The authority of the past, constantly dwindling under pressures of economic innovation in the First World, sinks in another way with demographic explosion in the Third World, as fresh generations of the living come to outnumber all the legions of the dead. This expansion of the bounds of capital inevitably dilutes its stocks of inherited culture. The result is a characteristic drop in 'level' with the postmodern. The culture of modernism was inescapably elitist: produced by isolated exiles, disaffected minorities, intransigent vanguards. An art cast in heroic mould, it was constitutively oppositional: not simply flouting conventions of taste, but more significantly, defying the solicitations of the market.

The culture of postmodernism, Jameson has argued, is by contrast far more demotic. For here another and more sweeping sort of de-differentiation has been at work. The bypassing of borders between the fine arts has usually been a gesture in the unaccommodating tradition of the avant-garde. The dissolution of frontiers between 'high' and 'low' genres in the culture at large, celebrated by Fiedler already at the end of the sixties, answered to a different logic. From the start, its direction was unequivocally populist. In this respect the postmodern has been marked by new patterns of both consumption and production. On the one hand, for example, leading works of fiction – boosted by lavish advertising and prize-publicity – could regularly hit the best-seller lists, if not the wide screen, in a way earlier impossible. On the other, a significant range of hitherto excluded groups – women, ethnic and other minorities, immigrants – gained access to the postmodern forms, broadening the basis of artistic output considerably. In quality, some levelling effect was undeniable: the time of the great individual signatures and master-works of modernism was over. In part this reflected an overdue reaction against norms of charisma that were now anachronistic. But it also expressed a new relation to the market – the extent to which this was a culture of accompaniment, rather than antagonism, to the economic order.

Therein, however, lay precisely the power of the postmodern.

Whereas in its heyday modernism had never been much more than an enclave, Jameson points out, postmodernism is now hegemonic. This did not mean it exhausts the field of cultural production. Any hegemony, as Raymond Williams insisted, was a 'dominant' rather than a total system, one virtually ensuring – because of its selective definitions of reality – the coexistence of 'residual' and 'emergent' forms resistant to it. Postmodernism was a dominant of this kind, and no more. But that was vast enough. For this hegemony was no local affair. For the first time, it was tendentially global in scope. Not as a pure common denominator of the advanced capitalist societies, however, but as the projection of the power of one of them. 'Postmodernism may be said to be the first specifically North American global style'.[14]

If these were the principal coordinates of the postmodern, what was the appropriate stance towards it? Jameson's final move was perhaps the most original of all. Hitherto, it could be said that every significant contribution to the idea of postmodernity had carried a strong – negative or positive – valuation of it. The antithetical judgements of Levin and Fiedler, the late Hassan and Jencks, Habermas and Lyotard, offer a set pattern. From a range of distinct political standpoints, the critic could either lament the advent of the postmodern as a corruption of the modern, or celebrate it as an emancipation. Very early on – soon after his Whitney lecture – Jameson mapped out an ingenious combinatory of such oppositions in 'Theories of the Postmodern', reproduced in *The Cultural Turn*. The purpose of his exercise was to point the way out of this closed, repetitive space. Jameson's own political commitments were well to the left of any of the figures charted within it. He alone had firmly identified postmodernism with a new stage of capitalism, understood in classical Marxist terms. But mere excoriation was no more fruitful than adhesion. Another kind of purchase was needed.

The temptation to be avoided, above all, was moralism. The complicity of postmodernism with the logic of the market and of the spectacle was unmistakeable. But simple condemnation

[14] *Postmodernism*, p. 20.

of it as a culture was sterile. Again and again – to the surprise
of many, on left and right alike – Jameson has insisted on the
futility of moralizing about the rise of the postmodern. However
accurate might be the local judgements it delivered, such moralism was an 'impoverished luxury' that a historical view could
not afford.[15] In this, Jameson was faithful to long-held convic-
tions. Ethical doctrines presupposed a certain social homo-
geneity, in which they could rewrite institutional exigencies as
interpersonal norms, and thereby repress political realities in
'the archaic categories of good and evil, long since unmasked
by Nietzsche as the sedimented traces of power relationships'.
Well before addressing himself to the postmodern, he had
defined the position from which he would view it: 'ethics,
wherever it makes its reappearance, may be taken as the sign of
an intent to mystify, and in particular to replace the complex
and ambivalent judgements of a more properly political and
dialectical perspective with the comfortable simplifications of a
binary myth'.[16]

These remarks were aimed at a conventional moralism of the
right. But they applied no less to a moralism of the left, that
sought to dismiss or reject postmodernism *en bloc*. Moral
categories were binary codes of individual conduct; projected
onto the cultural plane, they were intellectually and politically
disabling. Nor were the tropes of *Kulturkritik* of any greater
avail, with their tacit flight to the imaginary of one or other
idyllic past, from whose balcony a fallen present could be
reproved. The enterprise on which Jameson had embarked – he
stressed that it required many hands – was something else. A
genuine critique of postmodernism could not be an ideological
refusal of it. Rather the dialectical task was to work our way so
completely through it, that our understanding of the time would
emerge transformed on the side. A totalizing comprehension of
the new unlimited capitalism – a theory adequate to the global
scale of its connexions and disjunctions – remained the unre-
nouncable Marxist project. It precluded manichean responses

[15] *Postmodernism*, p. 62.
[16] *Fables of Aggression – Wyndham Lewis, the Modernist as Fascist*, Berkeley and
Los Angeles 1979, p. 56.

to the postmodern. To critics on the left inclined to suspect him of accommodation, Jameson replied with equanimity. The collective agency necessary to confront this disorder was still missing; but a condition of its emergence was the ability to grasp it from within, as a system.

Outcomes

With these parameters in place, a coherent account of postmodernity had arrived. Henceforward, one great vision commands the field, setting the terms of theoretical opposition in the most striking imaginable way. It is a normal fate of strategic concepts to be subject to unexpected political capture and reversal, in the course of discursive struggle over their meaning. Characteristically, in this century, the outcome have been *détournements* to the Right – 'civilization', say, once a proud banner of progressive Enlightenment thought, becoming a stigma of decadence at the hands of German conservatism; 'civil society', a term of critique for classical Marxism, now a cynosure in the idiom of contemporary liberalism. In the dominion over the term postmodernism won by Jameson, we witness the opposite achievement: a concept whose visionary origins were all but completely effaced in usages complicit with the established order, wrested away by a prodigious display of theoretical intelligence and energy for the cause of a revolutionary Left. This has been a discursive victory gained against all the political odds, in a period of neo-liberal hegemony when every familiar landmark of the Left appeared to sink beneath the waves of a tidal reaction. It was won, undoubtedly, because the cognitive mapping of the contemporary world it offered caught so unforgettably – at once lyrically and caustically – the imaginative structures and lived experience of the time, and their boundary conditions.

How should we situate this achievement? Two answers suggest themselves. The first relates to the development of Jameson's own thought. Here there is a notable paradox. The vocabulary of the postmodern came, as noted above, relatively late to Jameson, after signs of initial reservation. But its problematic was there very early, and unfolds through successive works with astonishing continuity. In his first monograph, *Sartre – The Origins of a Style* (1961), written in his mid-twenties, he was already writing of 'a society without a visible future, a society dazzled by the massive permanence of its own institutions in which no change seems possible and the idea of progress is dead'.[17] Ten years later, in *Marxism and Form*, comparing the enchanted bric-a-brac of surrealism with the commodities of a postindustrial capitalism – 'products utterly without depth', whose 'plastic content is totally incapable of serving as a conductor of psychic energy' – he asked 'whether we are not here in the presence of a cultural transformation of signal proportions, a historical break of an unexpectedly absolute kind?'.[18]

Marxism and Form ended by observing that a new kind of modernism, articulated by Sontag and Hassan, had surfaced, which no longer – as an older modernism had – 'reckoned with the instinctive hostility of a middle-class public of which it stood as a negation', but was rather '*popular*; maybe not in small mid-Western towns, but in the dominant world of fashion and the mass media'. The films of Warhol, the novels of Burroughs, the plays of Beckett were of this kind; and 'no critique can have any binding force which does not submit to the fascination of all these things as stylizations of reality'.[19] A not dissimilar note is struck in *The Prison-House of Language*, where the 'deeper justification' of the use of linguistic models in formalism and structuralism lay not so much in their scientific validity, as in the character of contemporary societies, 'which offer the spectacle of a world of forms from which nature as such has been eliminated, a world saturated with messages and information, whose intricate commodity network may be seen as the very prototype of a system of signs'. There was thus 'a profound consonance between linguistics as a method and that systematized and disembodied nightmare which is our culture today'.[20]

[17] *Sartre – The Origins of a Style*, New York 1984 (second edition), p. 8.
[18] *Marxism and Form*, p. 105.
[19] *Marxism and Form*, pp. 413–414.
[20] *The Prison-House of Language*, Princeton 1972, pp. xviii–ix.

Passages like these sound like so many orchestral tune-ups for the symphony to come. But if they anticipate so directly leitmotifs of Jameson's presentation of the postmodern, there was perhaps another indirect presage of what lay ahead. From the start Jameson seems to have sensed a kind of petrification of the modern as a set of aesthetic forms, that drew his interest to authors who sidelined or manhandled them. The two novelists to whom he has devoted free-standing studies are Jean-Paul Sartre and Wyndham Lewis. One reason for his attraction to them is certainly that both were highly political writers, at opposite ends of the spectrum: iconoclastic Left and radical Right. Another, which he himself has stressed, is what Jameson calls the 'linguistic optimism' they shared – the confidence that anything could be expressed in words, provided they were untoward enough.[21] But equally important, and not unrelated, was the angle at which they stood to the mainstream of modernism – Lewis isolated by his mechanistic expressionism, Sartre by his reversions to the trappings of melodrama. Involuntarily in the one case (Lewis's subsequent neglect preserving, as in a time-capsule, 'a freshness and virulence' of stylization gone dead in the embalming of his great contemporaries), and voluntarily in the other (Sartre's deliberate waiver of the consecrated forms and 'passive-receptive vocations' of the high moderns),[22] these were writers who in their own fashion had already bumped against the limits of modernism. There was a time when Jameson thought some novel species of realism might emerge beyond them. But the space for a *salto mortale* into the postmodern was already being cleared.

Viewed biographically, Jameson's movement towards a theory of postmodernism thus seems virtually inscribed in his trajectory from the start – as if with the uncanny coherence of an 'original choice' in the Sartrean sense. But there is another way of looking at the same outcome. Jameson's writing on the postmodern belongs to a specific intellectual line. In the years after the First World War, when the great wave of revolutionary unrest in Central Europe had receded, and the Soviet state was

---

[21] *Sartre*, p. 204; *Fables of Aggression*, p. 86.
[22] *Fables of Aggression*, p. 3; *Sartre*, p. 219.

already bureaucratized and isolated, there developed in Europe a distinctive theoretical tradition that eventually acquired the name of Western Marxism. Born of political defeat – the crushing of proletarian insurgencies in Germany, Austria, Hungary and Italy which its first great thinkers Lukács, Korsch and Gramsci had lived through – this Marxism was separated from the classical corpus of historical materialism by a sharp caesura. In the absence of a popular revolutionary practice, political strategy for the overthrow of capital waned, and once the great depression had passed into the Second World War, economic analysis of its transformations tended to lapse too.

In compensation, Western Marxism found its centre of gravity in philosophy, where a series of outstanding second-generation thinkers – Adorno, Horkheimer, Sartre, Lefebvre, Marcuse – constructed a remarkable field of critical theory, not in isolation from surrounding currents of non-Marxist thought, but typically in creative tension with them. This was a tradition deeply concerned with questions of method – the epistemology of a critical understanding of society – on which classical Marxism had left few pointers. But its philosophical scope was not merely procedural: it had one central focus of substantive concern, which formed the common horizon of this line as a whole. Western Marxism was above all a set of theoretical investigations of the culture of developed capitalism. The primacy of philosophy in the tradition gave these enquiries a particular cast: not exclusively, but decisively, they remained true to the concerns of aesthetics. Whatever else it included, culture signified, first and foremost, the system of the arts. Lukács, Benjamin, Adorno, Sartre, Della Volpe formed the rule here; Gramsci or Lefebvre, with a more anthropological sense of culture, the exception.[23]

For all its common features as a tradition, Western Marxism was in many ways relatively unaware of itself. On the whole, its leading thinkers were scarcely apprised of each other across linguistic boundaries within Europe. The first work to afford an

---

[23] I have discussed the general background and character of this tradition in *Considerations on Western Marxism*, London 1976: for the latter trait, see pp. 75–78.

overview of its repertoire did not arrive till the early seventies, from America: and it was none other than *Marxism and Form*. Here, as in no previous text, the unity and diversity of Western Marxism were put on elegant display. If Jameson's book concentrated on Adorno and Benjamin, Bloch and Marcuse, Lukács and Sartre, leaving Lefebvre and Gramsci – each noted – aside, in this it kept to the promise of its title. The dominant strand of this descent was aesthetic. For the first time, one might say, Western Marxism was tacitly faced with its truth. What did such totalization, however, signify for the future of this tradition? There were many, including myself, who reckoned that the conditions which had produced it were now past, and other kinds of Marxism – closer to classical models – were likely to replace it.

This estimate was based on the renewed radical ferment in Western Europe of the late sixties and early seventies, and on the visible return of intellectual energies towards questions of political economy and strategy that had dominated the older agenda of historical materialism. The French upheaval of May 1968 could be seen as a revolving beacon of this change, flashing out the signal that Western Marxism was now overtaken, passing to the rank of an honourable legacy. A shrewder judgement saw the May Revolt in a somewhat different light, not as the end but the climax of this tradition. Peter Wollen's *Raiding the Icebox* is the only work whose power bears comparison with Jameson's as a route map of twentieth-century culture. A central episode in its narrative is the story of the Situationist International, the last of the historic avant-gardes 'whose dissolution in 1972 brought to an end an epoch that began in Paris with the Futurist Manifesto of 1909'. But Situationism, nurtured on Lukács, Lefebvre and Breton, was not only this. In theoretically igniting the explosion of May 1968, Wollen remarks, 'we can equally see it as the summation of Western Marxism'.[24] This was a more plausible reading. But its upshot was nevertheless quite similiar. The lessons of West-

[24] *Raiding the IceBox. Reflections on Twentieth Century Culture*, London 1993, p. 124.

ern Marxism, as of the classical avant-gardes, needed to be learnt and valued, but their time was up – 'a period has ended'.[25]

It is this verdict Jameson's work has so perfectly belied. His theorization of postmodernism, starting in the early eighties, takes its place among the great intellectual monuments of Western Marxism. Indeed, one could say that here this tradition reached its culmination. Arising once again from an experience of political defeat – the quelling of the turmoil of the sixties – and developing in critical contact with new styles of thought – structuralist, deconstructive, neo-historicist – far from Marxism, Jameson's work on the postmodern has answered to the same basic coordinates as the classic texts of the past. But if in that sense it is the continuation of a series, it is also a recapitulation of the set at a second level. For here different instruments and themes from the repertoire of Western Marxism are blended in a formidable synthesis. From Lukács, Jameson took his commitment to periodization and fascination with narrative; from Bloch, a respect for the hopes and dreams hidden in a tarnished object-world; from Sartre, an exceptional fluency with the textures of immediate experience; from Lefebvre, the curiosity about urban space; from Marcuse, pursuit of the trail of high-tech consumption; from Althusser, a positive conception of ideology, as a necessary social imaginary; from Adorno, the ambition to represent the totality of his object as nothing less than a 'metaphorical composition'.[26]

Such elements do not lie inertly together in forced combination. They are mobilized in an original enterprise which seems effortlessly to absorb them. Two features endow this work with its peculiar unity. The first is Jameson's prose itself. He once remarked that of the thinkers of Western Marxism, Adorno was 'the supreme stylist of them all'.[27] But there are times when any reader might wonder whether the description does not better, or at any rate more consistently, apply to himself. He opened his first book with the words: 'It has always seemed to me that a modern style is something in itself intelligible, above and

[25] Ibid.
[26] See *Marxism and Form*, p. 7.
[27] *Marxism and Form*, p. xiii.

beyond the limited meaning of the book written in it, and beyond even those precise meanings which the individual sentences that make it up are intended to convey.'[28] Future studies of Jameson's own writing could take this as a motto. For the moment, it is enough to note two features of a style of compelling splendour. The spacious rhythms of a complex, yet supple syntax – well-nigh Jamesian in its forms of address – enact the absorption of so many variegated sources in the theory itself; while the sudden bursts of metaphoric intensity, exhilarating figural leaps with a high-wire *éclat* all of their own, stand as emblems of the bold diagonal moves, closer to a poetic than analytic intelligence, with which this work unexpectedly cross-connects disparate signs of the total phenomenon in view. We are dealing with a great writer.

At the same time, Jameson's work on the postmodern unifies the sources on which it draws in a deeper substantive sense. The Western Marxist tradition was attracted to the aesthetic as involuntary consolation for impasses of the political and economic. The result was a remarkable range of reflections on different aspects of the culture of modern capitalism. But these were never integrated into a consistent theory of its economic development, typically remaining at a somewhat detached and specialized angle to the broader movement of society: taxable even with a certain idealism, from the standpoint of a more classical Marxism. Jameson's account of postmodernism, by contrast, develops for the first time a theory of the 'cultural logic' of capital that simultaneously offers a portrait of the transformations of this social form as a whole. This is a much more comprehensive vision. Here, in the passage from the sectoral to the general, the vocation of Western Marxism has reached its most complete consummation.

The conditions of this widening were historical. The view that the late sixties marked a critical break in the landscape of the Left was not altogether wrong. Intellectually, as the very title of his landmark essay and book indicates, Jameson's turn to a theory of the postmodern was enabled by Mandel's *Late Capitalism*, an economic study that situated itself in a classical

[28] *Sartre*, p. vi.

tradition distinct from any shade of Western Marxism. Empirically, economic life itself had anyway become so pervaded by the symbolic systems of information and persuasion that the notion of an independent sphere of more or less a-cultural production increasingly lost meaning. Henceforward, any major theory of culture was bound to encompass more of the civilization of capital than ever before. The traditional object of Western Marxism was enormously magnified. So Jameson's resumption of its heritage could yield a much more central and political description of the conditions of contemporary life than the precedents it drew on.

Crucial to the effect of Jameson's account here is its sense of 'epochality'. This way of reading the signs of the time owes much to Lukács. But Lukács's principal exercises in epochal analysis, *The Soul and Forms* and *The Theory of the Novel*, remain aesthetic or metaphysical. When he moved to the political, in his remarkable short study *Lenin*, Lukács defined the epoch that had opened with the catastrophe of the Great War as one stamped above all by 'the actuality of revolution'. When events disappointed this expectation, no further description could follow. It was then Gramsci, the thinker within Western Marxism from whom Jameson has taken least, who tried to capture the nature of the consolidation or counter-revolutions of capital between the wars. His notes on Fordism represent, in fact, the only real precedent in this tradition for Jameson's enterprise. It is no accident that they gave rise to so much discussion after the Second World War, or various attempts to sketch the features of a 'post-Fordism' in the seventies and eighties.

But, powerful and original (at times highly idiosyncratic) as they were, Gramsci's ideas about Fordism – embracing mass production, rigorous work-discipline and high wage-levels in the US, puritanism for lower orders and libertinage for upper strata, sectarian religion in liberal America and corporatist organization in fascist Italy – nevertheless remained laconic and unsystematic. In a sense, their 'epochality' too misfired. In many respects ahead of the time, behind it in a few, these jottings proved to be mainly suggestive after the event. Jameson's account of the postmodern contains no comparable insights into the labour process or production, relying as it does on a self-standing economic literature of its own. But it is, of course, enormously more developed and detailed as the definition of an epoch, and supported by contemporary experience. Yet much of the critical charge of this theory also comes from its tension with the very climate of time it depicts. For, as we read in the first sentence of *Postmodernism*: 'It is safest to grasp the concept of the postmodern as an attempt to think the present historically in an age that has forgotten how to think historically in the first place'.[29]

If, in all these ways, Jameson's work appears like a grandiose finale of Western Marxism, in another way it has significantly exceeded this tradition. Nurtured in Europe, the work of its major thinkers never moved far beyond it as an intellectual force. Lukács was known in Japan before the war, and in exile the Frankfurt School discovered the United States. Later, Sartre was read by Fanon and Althusser studied in Latin America. But essentially this was a Marxism whose radius of influence remained limited to the original core of the advanced capitalist world: Western not only in its origins and themes, but also its impact. Jameson's theory of the postmodern has broken this pattern. Its initial formulations were focused principally on North America. But as his work on the question developed, its implications widened: postmodernism, he concluded, was – not additionally, but intrinsically – the cultural ether of a global system that overruled all geographical divisions. Its logic compelled a major turn in Jameson's own field of enquiry.

Up to the eve of the eighties, Jameson's critical practice was exclusively literary and its objects eminently Western. Proust, Hemingway, Balzac, Dickens, Eichendorff, Flaubert, Conrad – such were the figures in the foreground of his attention. With the eighties, there is a sharp change. Visual forms start to compete with written, and rapidly come to predominate – a shift evident in *Postmodernism* itself. Simultaneously there is a striking movement outwards, to cultures and regions beyond the West. In this period, Jameson was to reflect on Soseki and Karatani in Japan; Lu Xun and Lao She in China; Sembène in

[29] *Postmodernism*, p. ix.

Senegal and Solas or Barnet in Cuba; Edward Yang of Taiwan and Kidlak Tahimik of the Philippines.[30] In *The Cultural Turn*, discussions can be found of the films of Paul Leduc, Mexican director of a silent movie set in Venezuela, and Souleymane Cissé from Mali. Is there any contemporary critic with an even distantly comparable range?

The sense of such interventions has been to encourage a 'geopolitical aesthetic' adequate to the enlargement of the cultural universe in postmodern conditions. This has been no engagement from afar. Jameson first set out his ideas on postmodernism comprehensively in a lecture course in Beijing in 1985, and published a collection on the subject in China some years before he produced one in America. His account of 'Postmodernism and the Market' was tested out in Seoul. We owe the major text on 'Transformations of the Image' to an address in Caracas. Settings like these were not a matter of chance. Jameson's theory of postmodernity has won a growing audience in countries once of the Third or Second World because it speaks of a cultural imaginary familiar to them, part of the web of their own experience. A Marxism so naturally at home in the great metropolitan centres of the South and the East is no longer restrictively Western. With this break-out from the Occident, the idea of the postmodern has come full circle back to its original inspiration, as a time when the dominance of the West would cease. Olson's visionary confidence was not misplaced; *The Kingfishers* could virtually be read as a brevet for Jameson's achievement.

But if that was possible, it is also because Jameson shared something with Olson that distinguishes him from the intellectual line from which he descends. In one crucial respect, Jameson's work departs from the whole tenor of Western

[30] See, respectively, 'Soseki and Western Modernism', *boundary 2*, Fall 1991, pp. 123–141; 'In the Mirror of Alternate Modernities', *South Atlantic Quarterly*, Spring 1993, pp. 295–310; 'Third World Literature in the Era of Multinational Capitalism', *Social Text*, Fall 1986, pp. 65–88; 'Literary Innovation and Modes of Production', *Modern Chinese Literature*, September 1984, pp. 67–72; 'On Literary and Cultural Import-Substitution in the Third World: the Case of the Testimonio', *Margins*, Spring 1991, pp. 11–34; *The Geopolitical Aesthetic*, London 1992, pp. 114–157, 186–213.

Marxism. That was a tradition whose major monuments were in one way or another, secretly or openly, all affected by a deep historical pessimism.[31] Their most original and powerful themes – Lukács's destruction of reason, Gramsci's war of position, Benjamin's angel of catastrophe, Adorno's damaged subject, Sartre's violence of scarcity, Althusser's ubiquity of illusion – spoke not of an alleviated future, but of an implacable present. Tones varied within a common range, from the stoic to the melancholy, the wintry to the apocalyptic. Jameson's writing is of a different timbre. Although his topic has certainly not been one of comfort to the Left, his treatment of it has never been acrimonious or despondent. On the contrary, the magic of Jameson's style is to conjure into being what might be thought impossible – a lucid enchantment of the world.

Its themes are as grave as any in the tradition. But a spray of wonder and pleasure – the chances of happiness in a stifling time – is never far from the swell of even the most ominous reflection. 'To move, to instruct, to delight'. If few other subversive thinkers have come so close to the aims of art, the reasons are no doubt in part contingent. Jameson can evoke bodily experience as memorably as Sartre, but the feeling-tone is habitually the opposite – nearer elation than disgust. The pleasures of the intellect and of the imagination are no less vividly rendered than those of the senses. The glow with which Jameson can endow objects, concepts, fictions is the same.[32] The biographical sources of this warmth are one thing. Its philosophical premises are another. Behind this consent to the world lies the deeply Hegelian cast of Jameson's Marxism, noted by many critics,[33] which has equipped him to confront

[31] For this aspect, see *Considerations on Western Marxism*, pp. 88–92.

[32] Perhaps the finest example is his essay on Godard's *Passion* in *The Geopolitical Aesthetic*, London 1992, pp. 158–185. The contrast with Adorno's treatment of the object-world, even at its most eloquent, is telling. Compare, on a very similar topic, the passage in *Minima Moralia* (p. 40) – itself of great beauty – on the casement window or gentle latch, and the slamming of car or frigidaire doors, with Jameson's reverie on the levitations of the Californian garage in *Signatures of the Visible* (pp. 107–108).

[33] See, notably, Michael Sprinker, 'The Place of Theory', *New Left Review*, No 187, May–June 1991, pp. 139–142.

the adversities of the epoch, and work through its confusions, with an intrepid equanimity all his own. Categories such as optimism or pessimism have no place in Hegel's thought. Jameson's work cannot be described as optimistic, in the sense in which we can say of the Western Marxist tradition that it was pessimist. Its politics have always been realist. 'History is what hurts, it is what refuses desire and sets inexorable limits to individual as well as collective praxis' – above all in 'the determinate failure of all the revolutions that have taken place in human history' to date.[34] But utopian longings are not easily repressed, and can be rekindled in the least predictable of guises. It is this note too – the subterranean persistence of the will to change – that has given Jameson's work its force of attraction beyond the precincts of a jaded West.

[34] *The Political Unconscious*, p. 102.

After-effects

The capture of the postmodern by Jameson has set the terms of subsequent debate. It is no surprise that the most significant interventions since his entry into the field have likewise been Marxist in origin. The three leading contributions can be read as attempts to supplement or correct, each in its own way, Jameson's original account. Alex Callinicos's *Against Postmodernism* (1989) advances a closer analysis of the political background to the postmodern. David Harvey's *Condition of Postmodernity* (1990) offers a much fuller theory of its economic presuppositions. Terry Eagleton's *Illusions of Postmodernism* (1996) tackles the impact of its ideological diffusion. All these works pose problems of demarcation. How is the postmodern to be best periodized? To what intellectual configuration does it correspond? What is the appropriate response to it?

Timing

The central question here is the first – the issue of periodization. Jameson's earliest critic on the Left had pointed out a loose joint in his construction.[1] If postmodernism was the cultural logic of late capitalism, should they not coincide fairly closely in time? Yet Mandel's *Late Capitalism*, on which Jameson based his conception of a new stage in capitalist development,

[1] See Mike Davis, 'Urban Renaissance and the Spirit of Postmodernism', *New Left Review*, No 151, May–June 1985, pp. 106–113.

dated its general arrival from 1945 – while Jameson put the emergence of the postmodern in the early seventies. Even if it could be argued that the full realization of Mandel's model did not come overnight, such a gap remained troubling. Callinicos and Harvey, writing at virtually the same time, drew opposite conclusions. Harvey, whose earlier work *The Limits of Capital* had outlined the most systematic and original Marxist theory of economic crises, argued that the advent of postmodernity, rightly located towards the beginning of the seventies, in fact reflected a contemporaneous break with the post-war model of capitalist development. With the recession of 1973, Fordism – undermined by increased international competition, falling corporate profits and accelerating inflation – had plunged into a long-delayed crisis of overaccumulation.

In response, a new regime of 'flexible accumulation' had emerged, as capital increased its room for manoeuvre across the board. The new period saw greater flexibility of labour markets (temporary contracts; immigrant and domestic sweating), manufacturing processes (outsourcing of plants; just-in-time production), commodity outputs (batch consignments), and above all of deregulated financial operations, in a single world market for money and credit. It was this restless, speculative system that was the existential basis of the various forms of postmodern culture, whose reality and novelty were not to be doubted – a sensibility closely related to the dematerialization of money, the ephemerality of fashion, the glut of simulation in the new economies. None of this amounted to any fundamental change in the mode of production as such – let alone to a long-term solution of the pressures of overaccumulation, which had still not undergone the necessary purge of a massive devalorization of capital. Nor, indeed, could flexible accumulation itself be described as universally dominant; more typically, it coexisted in mixed patterns with older Fordist forms, and even the shifts from one to the other were by no means always irreversible.[2] What had critically altered, however, was the position and autonomy of financial markets within capitalism, outflanking

---

[2] *The Condition of Postmodernity*, Oxford 1990, pp. 121–197. The even keel of this work is very impressive.

national governments, which spelt systemic instability of an unprecedented kind.

Callinicos, on the other hand, reversed this line of argument. While it was true that global capital was now more integrated than ever before, and possessed new degrees of mobility, this in no way added up to a 'break' in the history of capitalism. For national states retained substantial powers of regulation, as the ironic success of Reagan's military keynesianism in reflating the world economy in the eighties had shown. As for the other features of 'flexible accumulation', they were mostly exaggerated or mythical: the labour force was less segmented, batch production less widespread, the service sector less significant than theories of post-Fordism suggested – just as Fordism itself was an overblown notion, projecting a homogeneous dominance of standardized mass production that had never existed, save in a limited number of consumer durable industries. Similarly, postmodernism as a distinct set of artistic practices – let alone a cultural dominant – was largely a figment. Virtually every aesthetic device or feature attributed to postmodernism – *bricolage* of tradition, play with the popular, reflexivity, hybridity, pastiche, figurality, decentring of the subject – could be found in modernism. No critical break was discernible here either.

What could be observed was something different: namely a gradual degradation of modernism itself, as it had become increasingly commodified and integrated into the circuits of post-war capital. The sources of this decline, however, were to be traced in the first instance, not so much to larger economic changes, or any immanent aesthetic logic, as more directly to the political history of the time. Historically, modernism had reached its apogee with the cluster of revolutionary avant-gardes between the wars – constructivism in Russia, expressionism and *neue Sachlichkeit* in Germany, surrealism in France. It was the victory of Stalin and Hitler that finished off these movements. Analogously, postmodernism – aesthetically little more than a minor twist in the downward spiral of modernism, though ideologically of much greater significance – should be seen as a product of the political defeat of the radical generation of the late sixties. Revolutionary hopes disappointed, this cohort

modernism

had found compensation in a cynical hedonism that found lavish outlet in the overconsumption boom of the eighties. 'This conjuncture – the prosperity of the Western new middle class combined with the political disillusionment of many of its most articulate members – provides the context for the proliferating talk of postmodernism.'[3]

Such contrasted diagnoses, reached from common starting-points, pose the problem of situating the postmodern with some accuracy acutely. In a sketch of the origins of modernism in the European *Belle Epoque*, I once suggested that it was best understood as the outcome of a field of force triangulated by three coordinates: an economy and society still only semi-industrial, in which the ruling order remained to a significant extent agrarian or aristocratic; a technology of dramatic inventions, whose impact was still fresh or incipient; and an open political horizon, in which revolutionary upheavals of one kind or another against the prevailing order were widely expected or feared.[4] In the space so bounded, a wide variety of artistic innovations could explode – symbolism, imagism, expressionism, cubism, futurism, constructivism: some quarrying classical memory or patrician styles, others drawn to a poetics of the new machinery, yet others fired by visions of social upheaval; but none at peace with the market as the organizing principle of a modern culture – in that sense, virtually without exception anti-bourgeois.

The First World War, destroying the *ancien régimes* in Russia, Austro-Hungary and Germany, and weakening landowners elsewhere, modified but did not overturn this setting. European upper classes and their *train de vie* went on much as before; advanced forms of industrial organization and mass consumption – Gramsci's idea of Fordism – remained largely confined to the US; revolution and counter-revolution battled from the Vistula to the Ebro. In such conditions, avant-garde movements and forms of great vigour continued to emerge – Opojaz in

---

[3] *Against Postmodernism*, Cambridge 1989, p. 168.
[4] 'Modernity and Revolution', *New Left Review*, No 144, March–April 1984; reprinted, with a postscript (1985), in *A Zone of Engagement*, London 1992, pp. 25–55.

Russia, Bauhaus in Germany, surrealism in France. The caesura
came with the Second World War, whose outcome smashed the
old agrarian elites and their way of life across most of the
Continent, installed stable capitalist democracy and standardized consumer-durables in the West, and gutted the ideals of
revolution in the East. With all the forces that had historically
spurred it gone, the *élan* of modernism gave out. It had lived
from the non-synchronous – what was past or future in the
present – and died with the arrival of the purely contemporaneous: the monotone steady-state of the post-war Atlantic
order. Henceforward, art that still would be radical was
routinely destined for commercial integration or institutional
cooption.

Much could be said of this rapid outline, by way of expansion
or criticism, today. It invites more geographical nuance. What
determined the gradient of technological enthusiasm in the early
forms of modernism? Why was Britain seemingly so barren of
innovative movements – or was it altogether? Can surrealism be
regarded as simply the last in the series of major avant-gardes
between the wars, or did it also configure something new?
Answers to questions like these would have to look more closely
at the national specificities of the different cultures of the time.
Schematically, for example, one could envisage a spectrum of
ideal attitudes to the new mechanical marvels of the early
twentieth century, varying inversely with the extent of their
implantation: the two most industrially backward powers of the
continent, Italy and Russia, generating the most fervently tech-
nicist avant-gardes, in their respective futurisms; while
Germany, combining advanced industry in the West with the
retrograde landscape of the East, was split between expressionist
loathing and Bauhaus wooing of Metropolis; France, on the
other hand, with its pattern of modestly prosperous petty
production in town and country, permitted a quirkier synthesis
in surrealism, entranced precisely by the interlacing of new and
old. As for Britain, the failure of its flickering modernist
impulses to endure was surely related to the absence of any
major insurgent strand in the labour movement. But it was no
doubt also a function of early industrialization, and the gradual
development of an overwhelmingly urbanized but already

Post war modernism —
avant-gardes

tradition-bound economy, whose slowness acted as a buffer against the shock of a new machine-age that galvanized avant-gardes elsewhere.

But the more important limits of the account retraced above are to be found at the end rather than beginning of the story. The cut-off point proposed for modernism after 1945 was certainly too abrupt. Peter Wollen's history amply demonstrates that. The legacy of the pre-war avant-gardes could not be extinguished overnight, since it necessarily still stood as internal model and memory, no matter how unfavourable the external circumstances for reproducing it. In America, abstract expressionism offered a poignant illustration of the new situation. Formally an exemplary modernist gesture, the most radical collective break with figurality to date, the New York school went from garret to apotheosis at – comparatively speaking – lightning speed, marking something quite new in the history of painting. This was an avant-garde that became an orthodoxy in its own short life-span, capitalized as symbolic investment by big money and promulgated as ideological value by the state. Yet the Cold War trumpeting of this art by the USIA had a peculiar irony. Connexions with surrealism were vital in abstract expressionism, and the politics of its leading painters could hardly have been further from their use as a moral affiche for the Free World: Rothko was an anarchist, Motherwell a socialist, and Pollock – in the private opinion of Greenberg, his greatest public champion – nothing less than a 'goddam stalinist from start to finish'.[5]

In Europe, where the annexationist logic of the post-war art market was less overpowering, and significant forces of resistance to the Cold War system persisted in the West, continuities with the insurgent aims of the inter-war avant-gardes were much stronger. Surrealism could still trigger successive projects conceived more or less in its image, as Wollen shows in his detailed reconstruction of the movement from COBRA and *lettrisme* to the Situationist International.[6] Here, the heroic

[5] See T. J. Clark, 'In Defense of Abstract Expressionism', *October*, No 69, Summer 1994, p. 45.
[6] *Raiding the Icebox*, pp. 135–150.

Post-war
avant-gardes;
└ situationism; etc

ambition of the historic avant-garde – the transfiguration of art and politics alike – sprang to life once more. But even before the climax of 1968, the union had come loose. The artistic wings of Situationism were essentially a product of the periphery: Denmark, Holland, Belgium, Piedmont, where the gallery system was weak. The political head was centred in France, where revolutionary militancy and the art market were both much stronger, creating a field of suspicion within the International of which the artists paid the price, in expulsion or departure; condemning the SI in turn to the hazards, and transience, of any overpoliticization. Another great adventure of these years lasted longer. In some ways strangely parallel in trajectory, Godard's cinema moved towards steadily more radical forms – of narrative ellipse, torsion between sound and image, didactic caption – in the same period, throwing off a series of near-masterpieces, before culminating in a convulsive, unsustainable bid for a revolutionary ascesis in the aftermath of 1968. Later, Godard's withdrawal to Switzerland might be compared to Jorn's refuges in Liguria or Denmark: a different kind of productivity, once again of the margin.

The quarter century after the end of hostilities thus seems in retrospect an inter-regnum, in which modernist energies were not subject to sudden cancellation, but still glowed intermittently here and there, where conditions allowed, within an inhospitable general climate. It was not until the turn of the seventies that the ground for an altogether new configuration was prepared. If we want to fix the emergence of a postmodernism more accurately, one way of doing so is to look at what had replaced the principal determinants of modernism. Jameson's work, in fact, contains pointers to most of the relevant changes, which with the slightest of rearrangements afford the more precise focus required. Postmodernism can be viewed as a cultural field triangulated, in its turn, by three new historical coordinates. The first of these lies in the fate of the ruling order itself. By the end of the Second World War the power of aristocratic tradition had received its quietus across continental Europe. But for another generation, its traditional alter – rival and partner – persisted. We can still speak of the bourgeoisie as a class, in that meaning of the term in which Max Weber could remark with pride that he belonged to it. That is to say, a social force with its own sense of collective identity, characteristic moral codes and cultural *habitus*. If we wanted a single visual clip of this world, it was a scene where men still wore hats. The United States had its version in the old money of the Eastern establishment.

Schumpeter always argued that capitalism, as an intrinsically amoral economic system driven by the pursuit of profit, dissolvent of all barriers to market calculation, depended critically on pre-capitalist – in essence nobiliary – values and manners to hold it together as social and political order. But this aristocratic 'under-girding', as he put it, was typically reinforced by a secondary structure of support, in bourgeois milieux confident of the moral dignity of their own calling: subjectively closer to portraits by Mann than Flaubert. In the epoch of the Marshall Plan and the genesis of the European Community, this world lived on. In the political realm, substantial figures like Adenauer, De Gasperi, Monnet embodied this persistence – their political relationship to Churchill or De Gaulle, grandees from a seigneurial past, as if an after-image of an original compact that socially was no longer valid. But, as it turned out, the two braces in the older structure were more interdependent than they once had seemed.

For within the span of another twenty years, the bourgeoisie too – in any strict sense, as a class possessed of self-consciousness and morale – was all but extinct. Here and there, pockets of a traditional bourgeois setting can still be found in provincial cities of Europe, and perhaps in certain regions of North America, typically preserved by religious piety: family networks in the Veneto or Basque lands, conservative notables in the Bordelais, parts of the German *Mittelstand*, and so on. But by and large, the bourgeoisie as Baudelaire or Marx, Ibsen or Rimbaud, Grosz or Brecht – or even Sartre or O'Hara – knew it, is a thing of the past. In place of that solid amphitheatre is an aquarium of floating, evanescent forms – the projectors and managers, auditors and janitors, administrators and speculators of contemporary capital: functions of a monetary universe that knows no social fixities or stable identities.

Not that inter-generational mobility has greatly increased, if at all, in the richer societies of the post-war world. These remain as objectively stratified as ever. But the cultural and psychological markers of position have become steadily more eroded among those who enjoy wealth or power. Agnelli or Wallenberg now evoke a distant past, in a time whose typical masks are Milken or Gates. From the seventies onwards, the leading personnel of the major states was moulting too – Nixon, Tanaka, Craxi were among the new plumes. More widely, in the public sphere democratization of manners and disinhibition of mores advanced together. For long, sociologists had debated the *embourgeoisement* of the working-class in the West – never a very happy term for the processes at issue. By the nineties, however, the more striking phenomenon was a general *encanaillement* of the possessing classes – as it were: starlet princesses and sleazeball presidents, beds for rent in the official residence and bribes for killer ads, disneyfication of protocols and tarantinization of practices, the avid corteges of the nocturnal underpass or the gubernatorial troop. In scenes like these lies much of the social backdrop of the postmodern.

For what this landscape means is that two conditions of modernism have vanished utterly. There is no longer any vestige of an academicist establishment against which an advanced art could pit itself. Historically, the conventions of academic art were always closely tied, not only to the self-representations of titled or upper classes, but also to the sensibility and pretensions of traditional middle classes below them. With the passing of the bourgeois world, this aesthetic foil is missing. The title and site of the most deliberately lurid brat-pack show in Britain says everything: *Sensation* – care of the Royal Academy. Similarly, modernism tapped violent energies of revolt against the official morality of the time – standards of repression and hypocrisy notoriously stigmatized, with reason, as specifically bourgeois. The jettisoning of any real pretence of upholding these standards, widely visible from the eighties onwards, could not but affect the situation of oppositional art: once bourgeois morality in the traditional sense is over, it is as if an amplifier is suddenly cut off. Modernism, from its earliest origins in Baudelaire or Flaubert onwards, virtually defined itself as 'anti-bourgeois'. Postmodernism is what occurs when, without any victory, that adversary is gone.

86

modernism → role of
power =
Technology

A second condition can be traced to the evolution of technology. Modernism was powered by the excitement of the great
cluster of new inventions that transformed urban life in the
early years of the century: the liner, the radio, the cinema, the
skyscraper, the automobile, the aeroplane, and by the abstract
conception of dynamic machinofacture behind them. These
provided the images and settings for much of the most original
art of the period, and gave all of it an encompassing sense of
rapid change. The inter-war period refined and extended the
key technologies of the modernist take-off with the arrival of
the flying boat, the roadster, sound and colour on screen, the
autogyro, but did not add significantly to their list. Glamour
and speed became, even more than before, the dominant notes
in the perceptual register. It was the experience of the Second
World War that abruptly changed this whole *Gestalt*. Scientific
progress now for the first time assumed unmistakeably menac-
ing shapes, as constant technical improvement unleashed ever
more powerful instruments of destruction and death, terminat-
ing in demonstrative nuclear explosions. Another and infinitely
vaster kind of machinery, far beyond the range of daily experience, yet casting a baleful shadow over it, had arrived.

After these glimpses of apocalypse, the post-war boom
changed the countenance of the mechanical in more close-at-
hand and thorough-going ways. War production, above all – if
not only – in America, had converted technological innovation
into a permanent principle of industrial output, mobilizing
research budgets and design teams for military competition.
With peace-time reconstruction and the long post-war boom,
mass production of standardized goods integrated the same
dynamic. The result was an industrial version of Weber's
parabola of the spiritual: as the flow of the new became in its
very continuity a stream of the same, the charisma of technique
was transformed into routine, and lost its magnetic powers for
art. In part too this banalization reflected the absence, amidst a
ceaseless plethora of improvements, of any decisive cluster of
inventions comparable to those of the era before the First World
War. For a whole period the excitement of the modern tacitly
dwindled, without much alteration of its original visual field.

The development that changed everything was television.

This was the first technological advance of world-historical moment in the post-war epoch. With it, a qualitative jump in the power of mass communications had arrived. Radio had already proved, in the inter-war and war-time years, a far more potent instrument of social capture than print: not merely by reason of its lesser demands on educational qualification, or greater immediacy of reception, but above all because of its temporal reach. Round-the-clock broadcasting created potentially permanent listeners – audiences whose waking and hearing hours could at the limit be one. This effect was only possible, of course, because of the dissociation of the ear from the eye, which meant that so many activities – eating, working, travelling, relaxing – could be performed with the radio in the background. The capacity of television to command the attention of its 'audiences' is immeasurably greater, because they are not simply such: the eye is caught before the ear is cocked. What the new medium brought was a combination of undreamt-of power: the continuous availability of radio with an equivalent of the perceptual monopoly of print, which excludes other forms of attention by the reader. The saturation of the imaginary is of another order.

First marketed in the fifties, television did not acquire major salience till the early sixties. But so long as its screen was only black-and-white, the medium – whatever its other advantages – retained a mark of inferiority, as if it were technically still a laggard stepchild of the cinema. The true moment of its ascendancy did not come until the arrival of colour television, which first became general in the West in the early seventies, triggering a crisis in the film industry whose box-office effects are still with us. If there is any single technological watershed of the postmodern, it lies here. If we compare the setting it has created to the opening of the century, the difference can be put quite simply. Once, in jubilation or alarm, modernism was seized by images of machinery; now, postmodernism was sway to a machinery of images. In themselves, the television set or the computer terminal, with which it will eventually merge, are peculiarly blank objects – null zones of the domestic or bureaucratic interior that are not just inapt as 'conductors of psychic energy', but tend to neutralize it. Jameson has put this with characteristic force: 'These new machines can be distinguished from the older futurist icons in two related ways: they are all sources of reproduction rather than "production" and they are no longer sculptural solids in space. The housing of a computer scarcely embodies or manifests its peculiar energies in the same way that a wing shape or a slanted smokestack do'.[7]

On the other hand, image-resistant themselves, the machines pour out a torrent of images, with whose volume no art can compete. The decisive technical environment of the postmodern is constituted by this 'Niagara of visual gabble'.[8] Since the seventies, the spread of second-order devices and positionings in so much aesthetic practice is comprehensible only in terms of this primary reality. But the latter, of course, is not simply a wave of images, but also – and above all – of messages. Marinetti or Tatlin could erect an ideology out of the mechanical, but most of the machines themselves said little. The new apparatuses, by contrast, are perpetual emotion machines, transmitting discourses that are wall-to-wall ideology, in the strong sense of the term. The intellectual atmosphere of post-modernism, as doxa rather than art, draws many of its impulses from the pressure of this sphere. For the postmodern is this too: an index of critical change in the relationship between advanced technology and the popular imaginary.

A third coordinate of the new situation lay, of course, in the political changes of the time. The onset of the Cold War, after 1947, had frozen strategic boundaries and chilled all insurgent hopes in Europe. In America, the labour movement was neutered and the left hounded. Post-war stabilization was followed by the fastest period of international growth in the history of capitalism. The Atlantic order of the fifties, proclaiming the end of ideology, seemed to consign the political world of the twenties and thirties to a remote past. The wind of revolution, in which the avant-gardes had once skimmed, was gone. Typically, it was in this period, when most of the great experiments seemed over, that the notion of 'modernism' acquired currency

---

[7] *Signatures of the Visible*, New York 1992, p. 61; likewise *Postmodernism*, pp. 36–37.
[8] The phrase is Robert Hughes's: *Nothing if Not Critical*, New York 1990, p. 14.

politics

as a comprehensive term, to demarcate a canon of classical works to which contemporary critics now looked back.

Yet the outward appearance of a complete closure of political horizons in the West was still, for a whole period, deceptive. In continental Europe, mass Communist parties in France and Italy – and undergrounds in Spain, Portugal and Greece – remained unreconciled to the existing order; no matter how moderate their tactics, their very existence acting as 'a mnemonic device, as it were, holding the place in the pages of history' for the revival of more radical aspirations.[9] In the USSR, the passing of Stalin unleashed processes of reform that seemed in the era of Khrushchev to be moving towards a less repressive and more internationalist Soviet model – one committed to assisting rather than frustrating insurgent movements abroad. In the Third World, decolonization was shaking loose major bastions of imperial rule, in a series of revolutionary upheavals – Indochina, Egypt, Algeria, Cuba, Angola – that brought independence to much wider areas. In China, the established bureaucracy became the target of a movement orchestrated by Mao, invoking the ideals of the Paris Commune.

Such was the setting, with its mixture of realities and illusions, for the sudden kindling of explosive revolutionary energies among educated youth of the advanced capitalist countries – not merely in France, Germany or Italy, but equally in the United States or Japan – in the sixties. The wave of student revolt was rapidly, if more selectively, followed by labour unrest – most famously, the general strike of May–June 1968 in France, the Hot Autumn of Italy in 1969 and its protracted sequels, the miners' strikes of 1973–74 in Britain. In this great turbulence, echoes from the European past (Fourier, Blanqui, Luxemburg: not to speak of Marx himself), the Third World present (Guevara, Ho Chi Minh, Cabral) and the Communist future (the 'cultural revolution' envisaged by Lenin or Mao) criss-crossed to create a political ferment not seen since the twenties. In these years too, vital struts of the traditional moral order, regulating the relations between generations and sexes, started to give way. No-one has retraced the parabola of

[9] *Marxism and Form*, p. 273.

*politics — end
of revolt,
the new right*

that time better than Jameson, in his essay 'Periodizing the Sixties'.[10] Quite naturally, it saw lively avant-garde flames spurt up again.

But this conjuncture proved to be a climacteric. Within another few years, all the signs were reversed as, one by one, the political dreams of the sixties were snuffed out. The May Revolt in France was absorbed virtually without trace in the political doldrums of the seventies. The Czechoslovak Spring – the boldest of all Communist reform experiments – was crushed by the armies of the Warsaw Pact. In Latin America, guerrillas inspired or led by Cuba were stamped out. In China, the Cultural Revolution sowed terror rather than liberation. In the Soviet Union, the long Brezhnevite decline set in. To the West, here and there labour unrest persisted; but by the second half of the decade the tide of militancy had ebbed. Callinicos and Eagleton are right to stress immediate sources of postmodernism in the experience of defeat. But these setbacks were only a preamble to more decisive checkmates ahead.

In the eighties, a victorious Right passed over to the offensive. In the Anglo-Saxon world the Reagan and Thatcher regimes, after flattening the labour movement, rolled back regulation and redistribution. Spreading from Britain to the Continent, privatization of the public sector, cuts in social expenditure and high levels of unemployment created a new norm of neo-liberal development, eventually implemented by parties of the Left no less than the Right. By the end of the decade, the post-war mission of social-democracy in Western Europe – a welfare state based on full employment and universal provision – had been largely abandoned by the Socialist International. In Eastern Europe and the Soviet Union, Communism – unable to compete economically abroad or democratize politically at home – was obliterated altogether. In the Third World, states born from national liberation movements were everywhere trapped in new forms of international subordination, unable to escape the constraints of global financial markets and their institutions of supervision.

The universal triumph of capital signifies more than just a

---

[10] *The Ideologies of Theory*, Vol 2, pp. 178–208.

defeat for all those forces once arrayed against it, although it is also that. Its deeper sense lies in the cancellation of political alternatives. Modernity comes to an end, as Jameson observes, when it loses any antonym. The possibility of other social orders was an essential horizon of modernism. Once that vanishes, something like postmodernism is in place. This is the unspoken moment of truth in Lyotard's original construction. How, then, should the conjuncture of the postmodern be summed up? A capsule comparison with modernism might run: postmodernism emerged from the constellation of a *déclassé* ruling order, a mediatized technology and a monochrome politics. But, of course, these coordinates were themselves only dimensions of a larger change that supervened with the seventies.

Capitalism as a whole entered a new historical phase, with the sudden fade-out of the post-war boom. The underlying cause of the long downswing, with its much slower rates of growth and higher rates of inequality, was the intensification of international competition, relentlessly forcing down rates of profit and so the springs of investment, in a global economy no longer divisible into relatively sheltered national spaces. This was the hard meaning of the arrival of the multinational capitalism flagged by Jameson. The response of the system to the crisis yielded the configuration of the eighties: the battering down of labour in core regions, outsourcing of plants to cheap wage locations in the periphery, displacement of investment into services and communications, expansion of military expenditure, and vertiginous rise in the relative weight of financial speculation at the expense of innovative production. In these ingredients of the Reagan recovery, all the deteriorated elements of the postmodern came together: unbridled *nouveau riche* display, teleprompt statecraft, boll-weevil consensus. It was the euphoria of this conjuncture that generated, with punctual timing, the first real illumination of postmodernism. The economic turning-point of the Reagan Presidency came on 12 August 1982, when the American stock-market took off – the start of the feverish bull-run that ended the Carter recession. Three months later, Jameson rose to address the Whitney.

art & literat-
Modernism -
po...,
the avant garde

Polarities

If such may have been the conditions of the postmodern, what can be said of its contours? Historically modernism was essentially a *post facto* category, unifying after the event a wide variety of experimental forms and movements, whose own names for themselves knew nothing of it. By contrast, postmodernism was much closer to an *ex ante* notion, a conception germinated in advance of the artistic practices it came to depict. Not that it has ever been significantly adopted by practitioners themselves, any more than was modernism in its (retrospective) heyday. But there is still a major difference in the respective weight of the terms. The time of the modern was that of the unrepeatable genius – the 'high modernism' of Proust, Joyce, Kafka, Eliot; or the intransigent vanguard – the collective movements of Symbolism, Futurism, Expressionism, Constructivism, Surrealism. This was a world of sharp demarcations, whose frontiers were staked out by the instrument of the manifesto: declarations of aesthetic identity peculiar not only to the avant-gardes, but also in more oblique and sublimated style characteristic of writers like Proust or Eliot, that separated the elective ground of the artist from the *terrains vagues* beyond.

This pattern is missing in the postmodern. Since the seventies, the very idea of an avant-garde, or of individual genius, has fallen under suspicion. Combative, collective movements of innovation have become steadily fewer, and the badge of a novel, self-conscious 'ism' ever rarer. For the universe of the postmodern is not one of delimitation, but intermixture – celebrating the cross-over, the hybrid, the pot-pourri. In this climate, the manifesto becomes outdated, a relic of an assertive purism at variance with the spirit of the age. In the absence of any system of self-designations internal to the field of artistic practices themselves, however, the external unifier of postmodernism has acquired a contemporary salience modernism itself never had, as a comprehensive rubric for them all. The gap between name and time has closed.

This is not to say that there was no discrepancy at all. The history of the idea of the postmodern, as we have seen, starts well before the arrival of anything that would readily be

painting.

identified as a form of the postmodern today. Nor does the order of its theorization correspond to the order of its phenomenal appearance. The origins of the notion of postmodernism were literary, and its projection to fame as a style was architectural. But long before there were novels or buildings that answered to standard descriptions of the postmodern, virtually all its traits had surfaced in painting. Since the Belle Epoque, this had usually been the most sensitive seismograph of wider cultural changes. For painting is set apart among the arts by a distinctive combination of features, that amount to a special statute. On the one hand, in the scale of resources required as a practice, its costs of production are far the lowest (even sculptors use more expensive materials) – a mere minimum of paint and canvas, within reach of the most indigent producer. By comparison, the capital sums needed for architecture or film are enormous, while writing or composing normally demands quite sizeable outlays to reach publication or performance. Another way of putting this is simply to note that the painter is in principle the only fully independent producer, who as a rule needs no further intermediation to realize a work of art.

On the other hand – and in dramatic contrast – the market for paintings involves potentially the highest rates of return on initial investment of any of the arts. Since the Second World War, the gallery system and auction room have steadily escalated values, towards astronomic figures in the top range. What is peculiar about the art market, of course, and explains these dizzying prices, is its speculative character. Here works can be bought and sold as pure commodities in a futures market, for profit to come. The two opposite sides of the situation of painting are, of course, inter-related. A picture is cheap to produce, because it involves no techniques of reproduction – no crane or steel, no camera or studio, no orchestra, no printing-press. But precisely for that reason, as what is non-reproducible – that is: unique – it can become incommensurately valuable. This paradox is joined by another within the practice of painting itself. In no other art is the barrier to formal innovation so low. The constraints of verbal intelligibility, let alone the laws of engineering, are far more rigid than the habits of the eye. Even music, dependent on specialized skills of the ear, is less free, as the infinitely smaller audience for modernist experiment in the medium of sound makes clear.

It is thus no accident that painting started to break with the conventions of representation well before any other art, even poetry, and has witnessed far the largest number of formal revolutions since. In front of the canvas, the painter enjoys an individual freedom without precise counterpart. Yet, far from being the pursuit *par excellence* of solitaries, painting has been objectively the most collaborative of modern arts. In no other do the terms 'school' and 'movement' – in the strong sense of mutual learning and common purpose – recur so frequently and actively. Originally, training in the academy or studio was no doubt critical for this. But perhaps too, at some deeper level, the very liberty of painting, in its unnerving space of invention, has needed the compensation of a distinctive sociability. At all events, painters have typically consorted with each other as writers or musicians have rarely done, and in their interaction have furnished much the clearest series of stylistic breaks in the general history of modernism.

These features marked painting out in advance as likely to be the privileged site for a transition to the postmodern. The last major school of the modern, abstract expressionism, had been the first to hit a zenith of current success. But what the market gave, it took away. As Greenberg noted: 'In the spring of 1962 there came the sudden collapse, market-wise and publicity-wise, of Abstract Expressionism as a collective manifestation' – a débâcle 'touched off by the long stock-market decline of the winter and spring of 1962, which had nothing to do with art intrinsically'.[11] Six months later, New York saw the triumph of Pop Art in the fall. Originally, the new style had strong links to a radical past. Rauschenberg had taught under Albers and Olson at Black Mountain, and enjoyed close ties with Duchamp and Cage; Johns was initially hailed as a neo-Dada. Fascination with the machine-made daily environment was a return to one of the oldest avant-garde interests. But by the sixties, this already appeared as an impulse with a difference. Few real machines

[11] Clement Greenberg, *The Collected Essays and Criticism*, Vol 4, Chicago 1993, pp. 215, 179.

figured in this painting, though the exceptions – Rosenquist's sleek nacelle of death – are suggestive. The characteristic icons of Pop Art were no longer mechanical objects themselves, but their commercial facsimiles. This art of cartoon-strips, brand-names, pin-ups, glazed banners and blurred idols supplied, as David Antin remarked of Warhol in 1966, 'a series of images of images'.[12] Citing the phrase two years later, Leo Steinberg was perhaps the first to dub this painting postmodernist.

With the later Warhol, indeed, a full postmodern has unquestionably arrived: nonchalant crossing of forms – graphics, painting, photography, film, journalism, popular music; calculated embrace of the market; heliotropic bending towards media and power. Here the curve deplored by Hassan, from a discipline of silence to a badinage of the dead-pan, was virtually traced within a single style – even so, not without all subversive effect. But if Pop Art offers one parabola of the postmodern, as it moved towards an aesthetic of flirtation, the movements that succeeded it took a more uncompromising orientation. Minimalism, launched in 1965–66, defied any easy appeal to the eye, not by a mixing of forms but by undermining the distinctions between them: initially, with the production of objects that were neither painting nor sculpture (Judd), then with the migration of sculpture towards landscape or architecture (Smithson, Morris). Here a characteristic modernist attack on perceptual conventions was radicalized in two directions, as spatial constructs were rendered temporal experiences, and institutional displays frustrated by site-binding.

Conceptualism, following hard on the heels of Minimalism – its first articulations came around 1967 – went further, dismantling the artistic object itself by interrogation of the codes constituting it as such. Coinciding with the height of the anti-war movement and the wave of urban uprisings in America at the end of the sixties, conceptualism was much more political in intention, mobilizing text against image for resistance not only

---

[12] 'The consequence of a series of regressions from some initial image of the real world': 'Warhol: the Silver Tenement', *Artnews*, Summer 1966, p. 58. Steinberg discussed this passage in *Other Criteria*, New York 1972, p. 91, where he characterized the 'all-purpose picture plane' of Rauschenberg as the basis of a 'post-Modernist painting'.

to traditional ideologies of the aesthetic in the narrow sense, but also to the contemporary culture of the spectacle at large. It was also far more international – America enjoying a brief priority, but no hegemony, as variants of conceptual art arose independently all over the world, from Japan or Australia to Eastern Europe or Latin America.[13] In this sense, conceptualism could be considered the first global avant-garde: the moment at which the fire-curtains of modern – euro-american – art parted, to reveal the stage of the postmodern. But conceptualism was this in another sense too. The formalist canvas was not just displaced by unclassifiable objects, eluding the system of the fine arts. Painting itself was deposed as the acme of the visual, and volatilized into other forms. Ahead lay the emergence of installation art. The pictorial is still suspended in the after-shock of this upheaval.

The break between the modern and postmodern thus not only came earlier in painting or sculpture than in any other medium, but was more drastic – a radical disturbance of the nature of the arts themselves. It is thus no surprise that it was precisely this area that gave rise to the most vaulting theories of the destiny of the aesthetic. In 1983, the German art historian Hans Belting published *Das Ende der Kunstgeschichte?*; a year later, the American philosopher Arthur Danto his essay 'The Death of Art'.[14] The close convergence of their themes has found further expression in Belting's enlarged second edition of his work, *Eine Revision nach zehn Jahren* (1995), which drops the question-mark in the first edition, and Danto's *After the End of Art* (1997).

Belting's original thesis took the form of a double attack: on

---

[13] The best account of the origins and effects of the movement is Peter Wollen's 'Global Conceptualism' (forthcoming). For a critique of its upshot, see Benjamin's Buchloh's alternative version, 'Conceptual Art 1962–1969: from the Aesthetics of Administration to the Critique of Institutions', *October*, No 55, Winter 1990, pp. 105–143, which taxes conceptualism with a 'purging of image and skill, memory and vision' that paradoxically contributed to a reinstatement of the very 'specular regime' it sought to void. This argument is far from over.

[14] Danto's text formed the 'lead essay' in the symposium edited by Beryl Lang, *The Death of Art*, New York 1984: pp. 5–35 – the remainder composed of responses to it.

the regulative 'ideal notions of art' that had informed professional art history since Hegel, but whose origins went back to Vasari; and on avant-garde conceptions of continuous 'progress' in modern art. These two discourses, he argued, had always been disjoined, since art historians – with the rarest of exceptions – had never had much to say about the art of their time, while the avant-gardes tended to reject the art of the past *en bloc* anyway. But both were historical mystifications. There was neither a unitary essence nor an unfolding logic in art, which not only assumed widely diverse forms, but fulfilled radically different functions, in the various societies and epochs of human history.

In the West, the dominance of easel painting dated only from the Renaissance, and was now over. Amid the disintegration of its traditional genres, it was now legitimate to ask whether Western art had not reached the kind of exhaustion in which the classical art-forms of East Asia were often on their home ground felt to have come to an end. At all events, it was clear that no coherent 'history of art' – that is, its Western variants, since a universal history had never been on offer – was any longer possible, only discrete enquiries into particular episodes of the past; and that there could be no such thing as a constant 'work of art' as a singular phenomenon, susceptible of a universally valid act of interpretation. In due course, Belting proceeded to a voluminous illustration of his argument in *Bild und Kult* (1990), a study of devotional representations from late Antiquity to the end of the Middle Ages, tracing 'a history of the image before the era of art'.

When he came to review his case in the mid-nineties, Belting no longer had any doubt that art history as once understood was finished. His attention now turned to the fate of art itself. Once, art was understood as an image of reality, of which art history furnished the frame. In the contemporary epoch, however, art had escaped its frame. Traditional definitions could no longer enclose it, as new forms and practices proliferated, not merely taking mass media as their materials, but often delivered by the electronic media themselves or even by fashion, as stylistic rivals of what remained of the *beaux arts*. The visual practices of this postmodern scene had to be explored in the

Danto/
pan

same ethnographic spirit as pre-modern icons, without commitment to any science of the beautiful appearance. In the nineteenth century Hegel had declared the end of art, and at the same stroke founded a new discourse of art history. Today, for Belting, we observe the end of a linear art history, as art takes leave of its definitions. The result is the opposite of a closure: an unprecedented and welcome openness marks the time.

Danto arrives at the same affirmation, by a slightly – albeit piquantly – different route. Here the 'end of art' is more philosophically announced, as the collapse of all master-narratives that lent the disparate works of the past a cumulative meaning. But such invocation of Lyotard by no means signifies similarity of deduction. The narrative whose death Danto wishes to celebrate is Greenberg's account of the dynamic of modern painting, moving by successive purges beyond figuration, depth, impasto to sheer flatness and colour. Its funeral was Pop Art, which in one variant or another unexpectedly restored virtually everything Greenberg had declared spent. For Danto, Pop Art marked the entry of painting into a 'post-historical' liberty, in which anything visible could become a work of art – a moment of which Warhol's Brillo Box could stand as the epiphany. For Pop Art was not simply a salutary 'adoration of the commonplace', after the elitist metaphysics of abstract expressionism (with its suspect links to surrealism). It was also a demonstration – here the connexion with Duchamp was essential – that 'the aesthetic is not in fact an essential or defining property of art'. Since there was no longer any prescriptive model of art, a candy bar could be as acceptable a work of art, if so proposed, as any other.[15]

This condition of 'perfect artistic freedom', in which 'everything is permitted', did not, however, contradict Hegel's *Aesthetic* but on the contrary realized it. For 'the end of art consists in the coming to awareness of the true philosophical nature of art' – that is, art passes over into philosophy (as Hegel said it

---

[15] *After the End of Art*, Princeton 1997, pp. 112, 185: 'A candy bar that is a work of art need not be some especially good candy bar. It just has to be a candy bar produced with the intention that it be art. One can still eat it since its edibility is consistent with its being art'.

must) at the moment at which only an intellectual decision can determine what is or is not art. This is an end-state which Danto explicitly associates with that other Hegelian prospect, the end of history as such, as reworked by Kojève. If the latter has not necessarily yet been reached, the former gives us a happy prevision of it. 'How wonderful it would be to believe that the pluralistic art world of the historical present is a harbinger of political things to come!'[16] Belting's construction – this is its principal contrast with Danto's – dispatches rather than appeals to Hegel. Yet it strikes a very similar note, at precisely this point, where the theme of a post-historical condition transmitted by Henri De Man to Gehlen, from the alternative source of Cournot, recurs at the same junction: 'The *Posthistoire* of artists, I want to argue, started earlier and has unfolded more creatively than the *Posthistoire* of historical thinkers'.[17]

The intellectual fragility of these interlocking arguments is evident enough. The equation of pre-modern icons with post-modern simulacra, as art before and after art, involves an obvious paralogism – since in the first case objects are endowed retrospectively with aesthetic status, while in the second they are expressly denied it. What qualifies, then, the latter as art at all? For Danto, the answer is essentially the fiat of the artist. The difference between the commodity in the supermarket and its reproduction in the museum lies in Warhol's debonair gesture itself. It would be difficult to imagine a philosophy of art that was, in substance, less Hegelian. The real inspiration here is closer to Fichte: the ego positing whatever world it wills. This paroxysm of subjective idealism is foreign to Belting, who proceeds with a more cautious anthropological step. But common to both theorists is a field-specific predilection. The postmodern is construed and admired essentially through its most brazenly ostensive forms: the emblematic artists are Warhol or Greenaway.

But the break can also be written in a very different way. For

---

[16] *After the End of Art*, pp. 12, 30–31, 37.

[17] *Das Ende der Kunstgeschichte. Eine Revision nach zehn Jahre*, Munich 1995, p. 12. I have discussed the intellectual origins of the idea of *Posthistoire* in 'The Ends of History', *A Zone of Engagement*, pp. 279–375.

AFTER-EFFECTS

Hal Foster, the most cogent theorist of a 'neo-avant-garde' indebted to its historic predecessors, but not necessarily inferior to them – indeed perhaps capable of realizing aims they missed – it is not the figurative wit of Pop Art but the austere abstractions of Minimalism that marked the moment of rupture: 'a paradigm shift towards postmodernist practices that continue to be elaborated today'.[18] For if the original avant-gardes had concentrated their fire on the conventions of art, they had paid relatively little attention to its institutions. In exposing these, the neo-avant-gardes had – as it were, after the event – consummated their project. This was the task undertaken by the cohort of artists whose work represented the most effective passage from minimalism to conceptualism: Buren, Brood-thaers, Asher, Haacke. The postmodern had never completely superseded the modern, the two being always in some sense 'deferred', as so many prefigured futures and reclaimed pasts. But it had inaugurated a range of 'new ways to practice culture and politics'.[19] The notion of the postmodern, Foster insists, whatever later misuses were made of it, was not one the left should surrender.

Such accounts appear virtually antithetical, not only in aesthetic but political accent. Yet the commonalities behind the contrasting norms of each are also plain. Parodically, one could say: without Duchamp, no Rauschenberg or Johns – without Johns, no Warhol or Judd – without Ruscha or Judd, no Kosuth or Lewitt – without Flavin or Duchamp (finally outflanked), no Buren. Even the last white hope of modernist abstraction, Frank Stella, once set up to be bulwark against everything sliding towards the postmodern, played a not inconsiderable part in its arrival. However the transformation of the visual is mapped here, connexions and oppositions are interwined. This history is still too recent for detached reconstruction, that would give all its contradictions their due. But a mere *ad hoc* nominalism is clearly insufficient too. The shifts in painting suggest a wider pattern. Some provisional way of conceptualizing what seems to be a constitutive tension within postmodernism is needed.

[18] *The Return of the Real*, p. 36.
[19] *The Return of the Real*, p. 206.

At the very origin of the term, as we have seen, there was a bifurcation. When De Onís first coined *postmodernismo*, he contrasted it with *ultramodernismo*, as two opposite reactions to Hispanic modernism, succeeding each other within a brief space of time. Fifty years later postmodernism has become a general term, whose primary connotations remain close to those indicated by De Onís, but which also visibly exceeds them towards the other pole of his construction. To capture this complexity, another pair of prefixes – internal to postmodernism – is needed. Perhaps the most appropriate could be borrowed from a revolutionary past. In a famous speech, on the 19th Nivôse of the Year II, Robespierre distinguished between 'citra-revolutionary' and 'ultra-revolutionary' forces in France – that is, moderates who wished to draw the Republic back from the resolute measures necessary to save it (Danton), and extremists who sought to precipitate it forward into excesses that would just as surely lose it (Hébert).[20] Here, purged of local polemic, is the dyad that more nicely conveys the polarity within the postmodern.

The 'citra' can be taken as all those tendencies which, breaking with high modernism, have tended to reinstate the ornamental and more readily available; while the 'ultra' can be read as all those which have gone beyond modernism in radicalizing its negations of immediate intelligibility or sensuous gratification. If the contrast between the pop and the minimal-conceptual in the postmodern gallery is archetypal, the same tension can be traced throughout the other arts. Architecture is a particularly marked case in point, where the postmodern stretches from the florid histrionics of Graves or Moore at one end to the deconstructive severities of Eisenmann or Liebeskind at the other: citra-modernism and ultra-modernism to monumental scale. But it would equally be possible to map – say – contemporary poetry in similar fashion. David Perkins's standard history, in effect, tacitly does so by distributing postmodern genres geographically, as between Britain and America –

---

[20] See F.-A. Aulard, *La Société des Jacobins. Recueil de documents*, Vol V, Paris 1895, pp. 601–604. No historian doubts that Danton and Hébert also belonged to the Revolution.

modernism exiting into Larkin or Hughes on one side of the Atlantic, and Ashbery or Perelman on the other. Enthusiasts for the latter, of course, would exclude the citra from postmodern poetry,[21] just as vice-versa Jencks would exclude the ultra from postmodern architecture. One of the most striking features of Jameson's critical writing is his effortless negotiation of both poles: Portman and Gehry, Warhol and Haacke, Doctorow and Simon, Lynch and Sokurov.

Does a formal divider of this kind correspond to any social demarcation-line? Confronting the culture of capital, modernism could appeal to two alternative value-worlds, both hostile to the commercial logic of the market and the bourgeois cult of the family, if from opposite standpoints. The traditional aristocratic order offered one set of ideals against which to measure the dictates of profit and prudery – a *sprezzatura* above vulgar calculation or narrow inhibition. The emergent labour movement embodied quite another, no less antagonistic to the reign of fetish and commodity, but seeking its basis in exploitation, and its solution in an egalitarian future rather than hierarchical past.[22] These two critiques sustained the space of aesthetic experiment. Artists in dispute with established conventions had the chance of metonymic affiliation with one class or the other, as moral styles or notional publics. Sometimes they were attracted to both, as famously were critics like Ruskin. There were also other options: the new urban petty-bourgeoisie – amiably popular, rather than gloweringly proletarian – was an important referent for the impressionists, or for Joyce. But the two principal zones of actual or imaginary investment were the upper atmosphere of titled leisure and the lower deeps of manual labour. Strindberg, Diaghilev, Proust, George, Hofmannsthal, D'Annunzio, Eliot, Rilke can stand for the first line;

---

[21] Compare David Perkins, *A History of Modern Poetry – Modernism and After*, Cambridge, Mass., 1987, pp. 331–353, with Paul Hoover (ed), *Postmodern American Poetry*, New York 1994, pp. xxv–xxxix. Were one to extend its scope beyond the arts, philosophy offers an obvious field for much the same contrast – Rorty at one end, Derrida at the other.

[22] For this duality, see in particular Raymond Williams, *The Politics of Modernism*, London 1989, pp. 55–57 ff.

Ensor, Rodchenko, Brecht, Platonov, Prévert, Tatlin, Léger, for the second.

Evidently enough, this divarication did not correspond to any particular pattern of aesthetic merit. But, equally plainly, it did indicate two opposite sets of political sympathies, that delimited the range of styles adopted on either side. There were, of course, significant exceptions here, like Mallarmé or Céline, where the hermetic and demotic exchanged ideological signs. But the general rule holds good that the field of modernism was traversed by two social lines of attraction, with formal consequences. How far can anything comparable be said of postmodernism? The departure of aristocracy, the evanescence of the bourgeoisie, the erosion of working-class confidence and identity, have altered the supports and targets of artistic practice in fundamental ways. It is not that alternative addressees have simply disappeared. New poles of oppositional identification have emerged in the postmodern period: gender, race, ecology, sexual orientation, regional or continental diversity. But these have to date constituted a weaker set of antagonisms.

Warhol can be taken as a case in point. In a sympathetic and ingenious reading, Wollen situates his 'theatricalization of everyday life' as a continuation of the historic avant-garde project of lifting the barriers between art and life, taken into the underground, where its political charge passed to gay liberation. But there is insufficient contradiction between this legacy and Warhol's later fascination with Reaganism – the phase of 'society portraits and cable TV'.[23] Subversive instincts were ultimately overpowered by something much larger. Wollen's authoritative rewriting of the overall trajectory of modernism stresses that at its origins lay a circulation between low and high culture, periphery and core, whose original outcome was much more disorderly and exuberant than the functionalist aesthetic later clamped down onto it, in the name of a streamlined industrial modernity, enamoured of Americanism and

[23] *Raiding the Icebox*, pp. 158–161, 208. For another attractive reading of the early Warhol, dating a decline from 1966, see Thomas Crow, *Modern Art in the Common Culture*, New Haven 1996, pp. 49–65: a volume that contains perhaps the best – aesthetically inclusive, yet historically trenchant – sketch of the original dialectic of modernism and mass culture in the visual arts.

Fordism. But, he argues, there always persisted a heterodox undercurrent of 'difference, excess, hybridity and polysemy' – occasionally visible even in such zealots of purity as Loos or Le Corbusier – which, with the crisis of Fordism, resurfaced in the decorative play of postmodern forms.[24]

At first glance, this looks like a story with an upbeat ending. Yet there are sufficient indications of new forms of corporate power elsewhere in Wollen's account to suggest a more ambiguous verdict. What is true, however, is that the institutional and technological complex to emerge out of the crisis of Fordism does not acquire the same proportionate weight as the Fordist configuration itself, in his reconstruction. The lesser detail allows a looser conclusion. The risk here is an understatement of the change in the situation of the arts since the seventies, where the forces at work in the revival of the ornamental and the hybrid have obviously not just been released from below. Another way of putting this would be to ask how far the appealing title of *Raiding the Icebox* is fully contemporary. Warhol's down-home phrase belongs to just that 'nostalgic elegy' for teenage years lived in a Golden Age of Americanism which, Wollen remarks, defined Pop Art as a whole. What could be more fifties than the refrigerator? Between such casual, haptic rifling among the preserves of the past and our postmodern present lies an electronic barrier. Today, scanning the picture-bank, surfing the net, digitalizing the image, would be more actual operations – all of them, necessarily, mediated by the oligopolies of the spectacle.

It is that transformation, the ubiquity of the spectacle as the organizing principle of the culture industry in contemporary conditions, which above all now divides the artistic field. The seam between the formal and the social typically lies here. The citra-modern can virtually be defined as that which adjusts or appeals to the spectacular; the ultra-modern as that which seeks to elude or refuse it. There is no way of separating the return of the decorative from the pressure of this environment. 'Low' and 'high' acquire a different sense here: denoting no longer the distinction between popular and elite, but rather between the

[24] *Raiding the Icebox*, p. 206.

market and those who command it. Not that, any more than in the modern, there is any simple correspondence between the relation of a work to the demarcation-line and its achievement. Aesthetic quality continues, as always, to be distinct from artistic position. But what can be said, with complete certainty, is that in the postmodern the citra inevitably predominates over the ultra. For the market creates its own supply on a scale massively beyond any practices that would resist it. The spectacle is by definition what mesmerizes the social maximum.

It is this endemic imbalance within the postmodern that surfaces in the after-thoughts of even its most serious and generous commentators. The last chapter of *The Return of the Real* has the melancholic title: 'Whatever happened to postmodernism?' – that is, the practices and theories its author had championed, now perceived as already flotsam, stranded on the banks of time by the onward stream of the media.[25] Wollen, viewing the Academy show of 1997, found installation art increasingly standardized in its hour of victory, and the spark of innovation unexpectedly passing back to painting, in doubtful combat with its new environment – or 'the tension felt in the art world between the legacy of a lost Modernism and the ascendant culture of the spectacle, the transformed and triumphal forces of eveything which Clement Greenberg dismissed as kitsch. The new world order is in the ascendant and the art

---

[25] *The Return of the Real*, pp. 205–206. It might be hazarded that Foster's remarks reflect a more general disappointment of *October*, the journal where they first appeared, whose key role in proposing radical versions of postmodern possibilities in the visual arts, after the path-breaking essays of Rosalind Krauss, Douglas Crimp and Craig Owens of 1979–1980, has yet to be properly documented. The collective volume edited by Foster in 1983, *The Anti-Aesthetic*, which included Jameson's Whitney address, is representative of this moment. For the change of tone by the late eighties, compare e.g. Patricia Mainardi's scathing 'Postmodern History at the Musée d'Orsay', *October*, No 41, Summer 1987, pp. 31–52. This is the trajectory that can already be found in Hassan or Lyotard. 'Citra' standpoints do not encounter the same difficulties – although on occasion perhaps they should. For an amusing example of imperturbable *suivisme*, applauding just what was originally decried, see Robert Venturi and Denise Scott Brown's complacent tale of the way the 'decorated shed' was wiped out by the 'duck' in their desert resort: 'Las Vegas after its Classic Age', in *Iconography and Electronics upon a Generic Architecture – A View from the Drafting Room*, Cambridge, Mass., 1996.

world cannot possibly insulate itself from it'. In this predicament, contemporary art is pulled in two directions: a desire to 'reassess the Modernist tradition, to reincorporate elements of it as corrective to the new Postmodern visual culture', and a drive to 'throw oneself headlong into the new seductive world of celebrity, commercialism and sensation'.[26] These paths, he concludes, are incompatible. In the nature of things, there is little doubt which is likely to bear the heavier traffic.

Inflections

Does Jameson's writing on postmodernism suggest any comparable evolution of emphasis? Similar notes are certainly struck in his study of Adorno, that can be read not only in the key of its title – *Late Marxism* – but also as a retrieval, in the spirit of Wollen's remark, of a dialectical legacy of late modernism. Jameson is explicit on this point: 'Adorno's modernism precludes assimilation to the aleatory free play of postmodern textuality, which is to say that a certain notion of truth is still at stake in these verbal or formal matters', and his example persists even at its most provocative. *Dialectic of Enlightenment*'s pitiless examination of Hollywood, whatever its other shortcomings, reminds us that 'perhaps today, when the triumph of the more utopian theories of mass culture seems complete and virtually hegemonic, we need the corrective of some new theory of manipulation, and of a properly postmodern commodification'.[27] In current conditions, what were once idiosyncratic limitations have become essential antidotes. 'Adorno was a doubtful ally when there were still powerful and oppositional political currents from which his temperamental and cantankerous quietism could distract the committed reader. Now that for the moment those currents are themselves quiescent, his bile is a joyous counter-poison and a corrosive solvent to the surface of "what is"'.[28] Here is the political voice of the same requirement.

[26] 'Thatcher's Artists', *London Review of Books*, 30 October 1997, p. 9.
[27] *Late Marxism – Adorno, or, the Persistence of the Dialectic*, London 1990, pp. 11, 143.
[28] *Late Marxism*, p. 249.

Jameson's book on Adorno is virtually contemporary with *Postmodernism, or, the Cultural Logic of Late Capitalism*. Since then, can we detect any inflection in his tracking of the postmodern? In the last part of the *The Seeds of Time* (1994), confessing 'a certain exasperation with myself and others' for over-stating the 'ungovernable richness' of the architectural forms of the postmodern, Jameson proposed instead a structural analysis of its constraints.[29] The result is a combinatory of positions, delimited by four signs – totality, innovation, partiality, replication – which forms a closed system. Such closure does not determine the responses of the architect to its set of possibilities, but does deflate the pluralist rhetoric of postmodernism. Still, it is striking that here Jameson professes admiration for all the practitioners or theorists – Koolhaas, Eisenmann, Graves, Ando, Moore, Rossi, Frampton – distributed round his semiotic square, no matter how mutually inimical. Consistent with this ecumenicism, although the social is often powerfully evoked in the course of the account, it affords no discrimination between positions, which are differentiated by formal criteria alone.

A paradoxical consequence is to find the embellishments of Moore or Graves aligned with the savage abhorrence of them by Frampton in the same aesthetic quadrant – which the analysis has then to decant into a subsidiary combinatory in order to separate out. Frampton, for one, might regard this way of looking at the architectural battlefield as insufficiently critical.[30] It is true that architecture occupies a peculiar position within the arts, which may help to explain Jameson's apparent reticence here. No other aesthetic practice has such immediate social impact, and – logically enough – none has therefore generated so many ambitious projects of social engineering. But since at the same time the cost and consequences of a major building complex are greater than those of any other medium, the actual exercise of free choice – of structures or sites – by the architect is typically smaller than anywhere else: overwhelmingly, clients corporate or bureaucratic call the shots. The very

---

[29] *The Seeds of Time*, New York 1994, p. xiv.
[30] Compare his *Modern Architecture – A Critical History*, London 1992, pp. 306–311.

first sentence of Koolhaas's enormous programmatic reverie, *S,M,L,XL*, reads: 'Architecture is a hazardous mixture of omnipotence and impotence'.[31] If a certain substantive impotence were the common base-line, then fantasies of omnipotence could only find outlet in forms.

It remains to be seen how far reasoning of this kind lies behind Jameson's approach. It is noticeable, however, that the combinatory – announced as only a sketch – has since been followed by interventions of more stringent cast, that start to pose the questions it left aside. An urbane review of Koolhaas's *summum* blends warmth of personal admiration for the figure with a forbidding projection of the future he extols – the disposable city, whose nearest anticipation is Singapore: an ebullient iconoclasm idealizing a virtually penitentiary setting, as the perverse destination of a 'vanguard without a mission'.[32] Subsequently, Jameson has insisted on the 'the agonizing issue of responsibilities and priorities' in contemporary architecture, and the need for a critique of its ideology of forms – where the facades of Bofill or Graves belong to the order of the simulacrum, and 'a wealth of inventiveness dissolves into frivolity or sterility'.[33] In the final text of *The Cultural Turn*, it is the speculative structure of globalized finance itself – the reign of fictitious capital, in Marx's terms – that finds architectural shape in the phantom surfaces and disembodied volumes of many a postmodern high-rise.

In other areas, the inflection looks sharper. Nowhere more so than in the stunning long essay on 'Transformations of the Image' at the centre of *The Cultural Turn*. Here Jameson registers a wholesale return within the postmodern of themes once theoretically proscribed by it: a reinstatement of ethics, return of the subject, rehabilitation of political science, renewed debates about modernity, and – above all – a rediscovery of aesthetics. In so far as postmodernism in a larger sense, as the logic of capitalism triumphant on a world scale, has banished

---

[31] OMA, Rem Koolhaas, Bruce Mau: *S,M,X,XL*, Rotterdam 1995, p. xix.
[32] 'XXL: Rem Koolhaas's Great Big Buildingsroman', *Village Voice Literary Supplement*, May 1996.
[33] 'Space Wars', *London Review of Books*, 4 April 1996.

the spectre of revolution, this recent twist represents in Jameson's reading what we might call a 'restoration within the restoration'. The particular object of his critique is the revival of a pronounced aesthetic of beauty in the cinema. Examples he discusses range from Jarman or Kieslowski at one level, through directors like Corneau or Solas at another, to current Hollywood action pictures; not to speak of the thematics of art and religion associated with the new output of the beautiful. His conclusion is draconian: where once beauty could be a subversive protest against the market and its utility-functions, today the universal commodification of the image has absorbed it as a treacherous patina of the established order. 'The image is the commodity today, and that is why it is vain to expect a negation of the logic of commodity production from it; that is why, finally, all beauty today is meretricious'.[34]

The ferocity of this dictum has no equivalent in Jameson's writing on architecture, which even at its most reserved is much more lenient on claims to visual splendour. What might explain the difference? Perhaps we should think of the contrasting position of the two arts – cinema and architecture – in popular culture. The first was virtually from inception its centre-piece, while the second has never really acquired much of a foot-hold. There was no filmic counterpart of functionalism. In this more rarefied field, a turn towards the decorative would be less tainted by immediate association with a long-standing aesthetic of entertainment than in the most come-on of all the commercial arts. In 'Transformations of the Image', Jameson takes his illustrations of the aesthetic of beauty from markedly experimental, calculatedly middle-brow and straightforwardly popular films alike. But if it is difficult to view *Latino Bar* or *Yeelen* in the same way as *Blue* or *The Godfather*, the pressure for their assimilation comes from the category of the last. This can be seen from the focus of Jameson's original attack on filmic beauty – the inauthentic 'cult of the glossy image' in box-office nostalgia pics, whose 'sheer beauty can seem obscene' as 'some ultimate packaging of Nature in cellophane of a type that an elegant shop might well wish to carry in its windows'. It is

[34] See *The Cultural Turn*, p. 135.

110

Jameson

notable that on that occasion, at the source of his objections, Jameson specified their opposite: those 'historical moments and situations in which the conquest of beauty has been a wrenching political act: the hallucinatory intensity of smeared colour in the grimy numbness of routine, the bitter-sweet taste of the erotic in a world of brutalized and exhausted bodies'.[35]

If those possibilities have so dwindled today, the reason lies in the 'immense distance between the situation of modernism and that of the postmoderns or ourselves' created by the generalized mutation of the image into spectacle – for today 'what character-izes postmodernity in the cultural area is the supersession of everything outside of commercial culture, its absorption of all culture, high and low', into a single system.[36] This cultural transformation, in which the market becomes all-inclusive, is accompanied by a social metamorphosis. Jameson's account of this change is, initially at least, more favourable. Pointing to greater levels of literacy and abundance of information, less hierarchical manners and more universal dependency on wage-labour, he uses a Brechtian term to capture the resultant levelling process: not democratization, which would imply a political sovereignty constitutively missing, but 'plebeianization' – a development which, with all its limits, the left can only wel-come.[37] But, as is often the way in Jameson, the dialectical depths of a concept disclose themselves only gradually.

Subsequent reflection on this alteration thus strikes a some-what different note. In *The Seeds of Time*, plebeianization reveals another aspect – not so much a closing of class distance, as a cancellation of social difference *tout court*: that is, the erosion or suppression of any category of the other in the collective imagin-ary. What once could be represented alternatively by high society or the underworld, the native or the foreigner, now fades into a fantasmagoria of interchangeable status and aleatory mobility, in which no position in the social scale is ever irrevocably fixed, and the alien can only be projected outwards into the replicant or extra-terrestrial. What corresponds to this figuration is not

[35] *Signatures of the Visible*, p. 85.
[36] See *The Cultural Turn*, p. 135.
[37] *Postmodernism*, p. 306.

any greater objective equality – which has, on the contrary, everywhere receded in the postmodern West – but rather the dissolution of civil society as a space of privacy and autonomy, into a jagged no-man's-land of anonymous marauding and deregulated violence: the world of William Gibson or *Bladerunner*.[38] Although not without its grim satisfactions, such plebeianization perforce denotes not greater popular enlightenment, but new forms of inebriation and delusion. Here is the natural soil of the luxuriant crescence of commodified imagery which Jameson analyses so powerfully elsewhere.

The notion of plebeianization comes from Brecht. But to register these ambiguities is also to recall a limit before which, we might say, his thought faltered. There was one massive reality Brecht's art never succeeded in rendering: the tell-tale sign of his uncertainty before it is the trivialization of *Arturo Ui*. For the Third Reich was also, undeniably, a form of plebeianization – perhaps the most drastic yet known, one which did not reflect but pursued the eradication of every trace of the other. To note this is not to conjure up renewed dangers of fascism, a lazy exercise of right and left alike today. But it is to remind us of an alternative legacy from that time, the example of Gramsci, who in his years in prison confronted the political strength and popular support of fascism without the smallest self-deception. It is in his notebooks that perhaps the most suggestive analogy for the social transformation of the postmodern can be found.

As an Italian, Gramsci was compelled to compare the Renaissance and the Reformation – the reawakening of classical culture and supreme flourishing of the arts his own country had known, and the rationalization of theology and formidable regeneration of religion it had missed. Intellectually and aesthetically, of course, the Renaissance could be judged far in advance of the Reformation that followed it, which – viewed narrowly – in many ways saw a regression to a crude philistinism and biblical obscurantism. But the Reformation was in that sense a conservative reaction that brought a historical progress. For the Renaissance had been essentially an elite affair, confined to

[38] *The Seeds of Time*, pp. 152–159.

Postmodernism as
'Plebianization'
of "culture"

privileged minorities even among the educated, whereas the Reformation was a mass upheaval that transformed the outlook of half the common people of Europe. But in the sequence from one to the other lay the condition of the Enlightenment.[39] For the extraordinary sophistication of Renaissance culture, confined to those above, had to be coarsened and simplified if its break-out from the mediaeval world was to be transmitted as a rational impulse to those below. The reform of religion was that necessary adulteration, the passage of intellectual advance through the ordeal of popularization, to a broader and so eventually stronger and freer social foundation.

The empirical qualifications required by Gramsci's account need not concern us here. What is pertinent is the figure of the process he described. For is not something very close to this the relation of Modernism to Postmodernism, viewed historically? The passage from the one to the other, as cultural systems, appears marked by just such a combination of diffusion and dilution. 'Plebeianization' in this sense does mean a vast broadening of the social basis of modern culture; but by the same token also a great thinning of its critical substance, to yield the flat postmodern potion. Quality has once again been exchanged for quantity, in a process which can be looked at alternatively as a welcome emancipation from class confinement or as a dire contraction of inventive energies. Certainly, the phenomenon of cultural coarsening, whose ambiguities caught Gramsci's attention, is on global display. Mass tourism, the greatest of all industries of the spectacle, can stand as its monument, in its awesome mixture of release and despoilment. But here the analogy poses its question. In the time of the Reformation, the vehicle of descent into popular life was religion: it was the protestant churches that assured the passage of post-mediaeval culture to a more democratic and secular world. Today, the vehicle is the market. Are banks and corporations plausible candidates for the same historical role?

It is enough to pursue the comparison a little to see its limits.

[39] Gramsci took much of his argument from Croce, but turned it more sharply in favour of the Reformation. For his principal reflections, see *Quaderni del Carcere*, Turin 1977, Vol II, pp. 1129–1130, 1293–1294; Vol III, pp. 1858–1862.

The Reformation was in many ways a social lowering of cultural heights previously attained: the likes of Machiavelli or Michelangelo, Montaigne or Shakespeare, were not to be reproduced again. But it was also, of course, a political movement of convulsive energy, unleashing wars and civil wars, migrations and revolutions, across the better part of Europe. The Protestant dynamic was ideological; driven by a set of beliefs fiercely attached to individual conscience, resistant to traditional authority, devoted to the literal, hostile to the iconic – an outlook that produced its own radical thinkers, at first theological, and then more openly and directly political: the declension from Melanchthon or Calvin to Winstanley or Locke. Here, for Gramsci, was the progressive role of the Reformation that paved the way to the epoch of the Enlightenment and the French Revolution. It was an insurgency against the pre-modern ideological order of the universal church.

The culture of the postmodern is the inverse. Although great political changes have swept over the world in the past quarter century, these have only rarely been the hard-fought outcome of mass political struggles. Liberal democracy has spread by force of economic example, or pressure – Marx's 'artillery of commodities' – not by moral upheaval or social mobilization; and as it has done so, its substance has tended to dwindle, both in its homelands and its new territories, as falling rates of voter participation and mounting popular apathy set in. The *Zeitgeist* is not stirred: it is the hour of democratic fatalism. How could it be otherwise, when social inequality increases *pari passu* with political legality, and civic impotence hand in hand with novel suffrage? What moves is only the market – but this at ever-accelerating speed, churning habits, styles, communities, populations in its wake. No predestined enlightenment lies at the end of this journey. A plebeian beginning lacks automatic connexion with a philosophical ending. The movement of religious reform began with the breaking of images; the arrival of the postmodern has installed the rule of images as never before. The icon once shattered by the dissenter's blow is now enshrined in plexiglass as universal *ex voto*.

The culture of the spectacle has generated, of course, its own ideology. This is the *doxa* of postmodernism that descends from the moment of Lyotard. Intellectually, it is not of much interest: an undemanding medley of notions, whose upshot is little more than a slack-jawed conventionalism. But since the circulation of ideas in the social body does not typically depend on their coherence, but their congruence with material interests, the influence of this ideology remains considerable – by no means confined to campus life alone, but pervasive in popular culture at large. It is to this complex that Terry Eagleton has devoted a scintillating critique in *The Illusions of Postmodernism*. At the outset, Eagleton distinguishes clearly between the postmodern understood as a development in the arts, and as a system of *idées reçus*, and explains that his concern is exclusively with the latter. He then considers one after another of the standard tropes of an anti-essentialist, anti-foundationalist rhetoric – rejections of any idea of human nature; conceptions of history as random process; equations of class with race or gender; renunciations of totality or identity; speculations of an undetermined subject – and, with delicate precision, dismantles each. There has rarely been so effective and comprehensive a dissection of what might be called, sardonically adapting Gramsci to Johnson, the common nonsense of the age.

But Eagleton's purpose is not just a *sottisier*. He would also situate the ideology of postmodernism historically. Advanced capitalism, he argues, requires two contradictory systems of justification: a metaphysic of abiding impersonal verities – the discourse of sovereignty and law, contract and obligation – in the political order, and a casuistic of individual preferences for the perpetually shifting fashions and gratifications of consumption in the economic order. Postmodernism gives paradoxical expression to this dualism, since while its dismissal of the centred subject in favour of the erratic swarmings of desire colludes with the amoral hedonism of the market, its denial of any grounded values or objective truths undermines the prevailing legitimations of the state. What explains such ambivalence? Here Eagleton's account hesitates. His study begins with the most sustained reading of postmodernism as the product of political defeat on the left ventured to date – a 'definitive repulse'.[40] But this is

[40] *The Illusions of Postmodernism*, Oxford 1997, p. 1.

presented as playful parable rather than actual reconstruction. For with characteristic sympathy, Eagleton suggests that postmodernism cannot be reduced to this: it was also the emergence of humiliated minorities onto the theoretical stage, and a 'veritable revolution' in thought about power, desire, identity and the body, without whose inspiration no radical politics is henceforward thinkable.[41]

The ideological ambivalence of the postmodern thus might be linked to a historical contrast: schematically – defeat of organized labour and student rebellion concluding in economic accommodation to the market, rise of the insulted and injured leading to political questioning of morality and the state. Some such parallelism is certainly latent in Eagleton's account. But if it is never quite spelt out, the reason lies in an equivocation at its outset. On the face of it, there would appear to be little common measure between the two background developments assigned to postmodernism: the one driven home in a frontal chapter that sets the scene for the whole book, the other – as it were – allusive compensation for it in a couple of paragraphs. Political reality would suggest that such a ratio was good sense. But it sits uneasily with the notion of ambivalence, which implies a parity of effect. Perhaps aware of the difficulty, Eagleton momentarily retracts with one hand what he advances with the other. The fable of political defeat concludes with the 'most bizarre possibility of all', as he asks: '*What if this defeat never really happened in the first place?* What if it were less a matter of the left rising up and being forced back, than of a steady disintegration, a gradual failure of nerve, a creeping paralysis?'. Were that the case, then balance between cause and effect would be restored. But, tempted though he is by this comforting fancy, Eagleton is too lucid to insist on it. His book ends as it begins, 'regretfully, on a more minatory note': not equipoise, but illusion is the bottom-line of the postmodern.[42]

The discursive complex that is the object of Eagleton's critique is, as he notes, a phenomenon that may be treated apart from the artistic forms of postmodernism – ideology as distinct from culture, in a traditional acceptance of these terms. But, of course, in a wider sense the two cannot be so cleanly separated. How, then, should their relationship be conceived? The *doxa* of the postmodern is defined, as Eagleton in effect shows, by a primary affinity with the catechisms of the market. What we are looking at, consequently, is in practice the counterpart of the 'citra' – as the dominant strand in postmodern culture – in the ideological field. It is striking how little concerned Jameson has been with it. But if we ask ourselves where the antithetical moment of 'ultra' theory is to be found, the answer is not far to seek. It has often been observed that the postmodern arts have been short of the manifestoes that punctuated the history of the modern. This can be overstated, as the examples of Kosuth or Koolhaas noted above indicate. But if aesthetic programmes can certainly still be found – albeit now more often individual than collective, what has undoubtedly been missing is any revolutionary vision of the kind articulated by the historic avant-gardes. Situationism, which foresaw so many aspects of the postmodern, has had no sequels within it.

The theoretical instance the avant-garde form represented has not, however, disappeared. Rather, its function has migrated. For what else is Jameson's totalization of postmodernism itself? In the epoch of modernism, revolutionary art generated its own descriptions of the time or intimations of the future, while for the most part its practices were viewed sceptically, or at best selectively, by political or philosophical thinkers of the left. Trotsky's coolness to futurism, Lukács's resistance to Brechtian *Verfremdung*, Adorno's aversion to surrealism, were characteristic of that conjuncture. In the period of postmodernism, there has been a reversal of roles. Radical strands in the arts, reclaiming or developing legacies of the avant-gardes, have not been lacking. But no doubt in part because of the disorienting coexistence of the citra-modern, of which there was no earlier equivalent, this 'ultra-modernist' culture has not produced any confident account of the age, or sense of its general direction. That has been the achievement of Jameson's theory of the postmodern. Here, viewed comparatively, is where the critical ambition and revolutionary *élan* of the classical avant-garde have passed. In this register, Jameson's work can be read as a single continuous equivalent of all the passionate meteorologies of the past. The totalizer is now external; but that displacement belongs to the moment of history that the theory itself explains. Postmodernism is the cultural logic of a capitalism not embattled, but complacent beyond precedent. Resistance can only start by staring down this order as it is.

Scope

The classical avant-gardes remained Western, even if the heterodox currents of modernism, of which they formed one stream, repeatedly sought inspiration in the Oriental, the African, the American-Indian. The scope of Jameson's work exceeds this occidental boundary. But it can be asked whether, in doing so, it nevertheless still projects an unduly homogeneous cultural universe at large, modelled on the North American system at its core. 'Modernism', writes Peter Wollen, 'is not being succeeded by a totalizing Western postmodernism but by a hybrid new aesthetic in which new forms of communication and display will be constantly confronted by new vernacular forms of invention and expression', beyond the 'stiflingly Eurocentric discourse' of the latter-day modern and postmodern alike.[43] The same kind of objection acquires more doctrinal form in the corpus of 'postcolonial theory'. This body of criticism has developed since the mid-eighties, largely in direct reaction to the influence of ideas of postmodernism in the metropolitan countries, and in particular to Jameson's own construction of the field.

The gravamen of the charge against his theory is that it ignores or suppresses practices in the periphery that not only cannot be accommodated within the categories of the postmodern, but actively reject them. For these critics, postcolonial culture is inherently more oppositional, and far more political than the postmodernism of the centre. Challenging the overweening pretensions of the metropolis, it typically has no hesitation in appealing to its own radical forms of representation or realism, proscribed by postmodern conventions. The

---

[43] *Raiding the Icebox*, pp. 205, 209.

champions of the postcolonial 'wish once and for all to name and disclaim postmodernism as neo-imperialist'. For 'the concept of postmodernity has been constructed in terms which more or less intentionally wipe out the possibility of postcolonial identity' – that is, the need of the victims of Western imperialism to achieve a sense of themselves 'uncontaminated by universalist or Eurocentric concepts and images'.[44] For this, what they require are not the pernicious categories of a totalizing Western Marxism, but the discrete genealogies of, say, Michel Foucault.

Postcolonial theory has already attracted a series of powerful rejoinders, which it would be otiose to repeat here.[45] The notion of the 'postcolonial' itself, as typically used in this literature, is so elastic that it loses virtually any critical edge. Temporally, its advocates insist, postcolonial history is not confined to the period since independence of states that were once colonies – rather, it designates their entire experience since the moment of colonization itself. Spatially, it is not restricted to lands conquered by the West, but extends to those settled by it, so that by a perverse logic even the United States, the summit of neo-imperialism itself, becomes a postcolonial society in quest of its breachless identity.[46] This inflation of the concept, tending to deprive it of any operational significance, no doubt owes much to its geo-political origins – which lie not where might be expected, in Asia or Africa, but in the former White Dominions: New Zealand, Australia, Canada; and perhaps something to its

---

[44] Simon During, 'Postmodernism or Postcolonialism?', *Landfall*, Vol 39, No 3, 1985, pp. 369; 'Postmodernism or Postcolonialism Today', *Textual Practice*, Vol 1, No 1, 1987, p. 33. These two texts from New Zealand, each of which takes Jameson to task, contain the earliest and clearest statement of key themes in this literature. For remarks on an 'underlying realist script' in postcolonial literature, see Stephen Slemon: 'Modernism's Last Post', in Ian Adam and Helen Triffin (eds), *Past the Last Post*, New York 1991, pp. 1–11, a contribution from Canada.

[45] See, in particular, Arif Dirlik, 'The Postcolonial Aura: Third World Criticism in the Age of Global Capitalism', *Critical Enquiry*, Winter 1994, pp. 328–356; and Aijaz Ahmad, 'The Politics of Literary Postcoloniality', *Race and Class*, Autumn 1995, pp. 1–20.

[46] See Bill Ashcroft, Gareth Griffiths, Helen Triffin, *The Empire Writes Back: Theory and Practice in Colonial Literatures*, London 1989, p. 2: the authors write from Australia.

intellectual sources too – the banalization of power in Foucault's overstretching of the concept comes to mind. At all events, a conception of the postcolonial as aqueous as this can scarcely affect its target.

A more reasonable construal of the term takes its prefix in less cavalier fashion, to denote a historical period where decolonization has indeed occurred, but neo-imperial domination persists – no longer directly based on military force, but on forms of ideological consent that call for new kinds of political and cultural resistance.[47] This version of the idea of postcolonialism clearly reflects more of the reality of the contemporary world, even if the second sign in the term still misses part of its target, since such major states as China – the specific object of this reinterpretation – or Iran were never colonized, and most of Latin America ceased to be so nearly two centuries ago. But in its insistence on the strength of market penetration of popular cultures outside the core zone of advanced capitalism, it goes far to meet – rather than contest – Jameson's description of the impact of postmodernism; indeed, at the level of detail, expressly confirms it. So, too, the vitality of mutant forms of realism in the arts of the periphery – where, say, employment of magical motifs can be seen as a typical resort to 'weapons of the weak' – and their unsettling effect, to which postcolonial critics legitimately point, does not contradict the configuration of the centre. There after all postmodernism, especially on its citra slope, always included certain realist appeals, and has had no difficulty in incorporating supernatural twists to them.

A more substantial objection to Jameson's case for a global dominance of the postmodern comes not from claims for the postcolonial, but rather simply from the lack of full capitalist modernization itself in so many areas of what was once the Third World. In conditions where the minimum conditions of modernity – literacy, industry, mobility – are still basically absent or only patchily present, how can postmodernity have any meaning? It is a long way from Diamond Dust Shoes to the

---

[47] See Shaobo Xie, 'Rethinking the Problem of Postcolonialism', *New Literary History*, Vol 28, No 1, Winter 1977 (Issue on 'Cultural Studies: China and The West'), p. 9ff.

Taklamakan or Irrawaddy. Jameson's argument, however, does not depend on any contention – obviously absurd – that contemporary capitalism has created a homogeneous set of social circumstances round the world. Uneven development is inherent in the system, whose 'abrupt new expansion' has 'equally unevenly' eclipsed older forms of inequality and multiplied new ones 'we as yet understand less well'.[48] The real question is whether this unevenness is too great to sustain any common cultural logic.

Postmodernism emerged as a cultural dominant in unprecedently rich capitalist societies with very high average levels of consumption. Jameson's first reconnaissance linked it directly to these, and he has since insisted further on its specifically American origins. Would it not therefore be reasonable to think that where levels of consumption were far lower, and the stage of industrial development much less advanced, a configuration closer to modernism – as it once flourished in the West – would be more likely to prevail? This was a hypothesis to which I, at any rate, was drawn.[49] In these conditions, might one not expect to find a pronounced dualism of high and low forms, comparable to the European divide between avant-garde and mass culture, possibly with a still wider gulf between the two? The Indian cinema would appear to offer a case in point: the contrast between Satyajit Ray's films and the avalanche of song-and-dance genres from the Bombay studios looking as stark as any in the developed world. But this, of course, is an example from a highly protected national market in the sixties. Today, global communications systems ensure an incomparably greater degree of cultural penetration of the former Second and Third Worlds by the First. In these conditions, the influence of postmodern forms becomes inescapable – in the architecture of cities like Shanghai or Kuala Lumpur, the art shows of Caracas or Beijing, novels and films from Moscow to Buenos Aires.

Influence, however, is not necessarily dominance. The presence of significant groups of artists, or clusters of buildings, whose references are clearly postmodern does not ensure any

---

[48] *Late Marxism*, p. 249.
[49] 'Modernity and Revolution', *A Zone of Engagement*, pp. 40, 54.

local hegemony. In the terms Jameson himself uses, after Raymond Williams, the postmodern could well be only 'emergent' – rather than the modern being 'residual'. This, certainly, is the view of such a level-headed critic as Jonathan Arac, surveying these issues in the country where they are more hotly debated than perhaps anywhere else today, the People's Republic of China.[50] With nearly a billion people still on the land, the conclusion is difficult to contest. It would be open to Jameson to reply that the global hegemony of the postmodern is just that – a net predominance at world level, which does not exclude a subordinate role at the national level, in any given case. However that may be, there is another consideration which must be weighed in the scales. Postmodern culture is not just a set of aesthetic forms, it is also a technological package. Television, which was so decisive in the passage to a new epoch, has no modernist past. It became the most powerful medium of all in the postmodern period itself. But that power is far greater – more absolutely disproportionate to the impact of all others combined – in the former Third World than it is in the First itself.

This paradox must give pause to any over-quick dismissal of the idea that the damned of the earth too have entered the kingdom of the spectacle. It is unlikely to remain isolated. For just ahead lies the impact of the new technologies of simulation – or prestidigitation – whose arrival is quite recent even in the rich cultures. We now have a strangely august diorama of these, in Julian Stallabrass's remarkable *Gargantua*. Here, quite unexpectedly, Jameson's call for a sequel to Adorno and Horkheimer's 'Culture Industry', to address subsequent forms of manipulation, has been fulfilled. No work since that famous analysis has so closely matched its ambition, or represented such a fitting succession; although here the countervailing influence of Benjamin tilts an Adornian project away from the declaratively systematic towards a more *pointilliste* phenomenal plane. Stallabrass surveys digital photography, cyberspace exchange and computer games – as well as a more familiar

---

[50] 'Postmodernism and Postmodernity in China: an Agenda for Inquiry', *New Literary History*, Winter 1997, p. 144.

landscape of automobiles, malls, graffiti, detritus, television itself – as prefigurations of a future mass culture that threatens to supersede the spectacle itself, as known hitherto, by effacing the boundaries between the perceived and the enacted altogether. With this development, the new techniques conjure the possibility of a self-sealed universe of simulation capable of veiling – and so insulating – the order of capital more completely than ever. A quiet gravity of tone, and precision of detail, characterize this unseasonable argument.

But its logic is in one significant respect at variance with its framework. Stallabrass will have little truck with any talk of the postmodern, and holds to a radical separation of rich and poor zones of the world – which, he suggests, it is one of the crucial functions of mass culture to mask.[51] But a more plausible deduction points the other way. The technologies he explores are in both timing and effect pre-eminently postmodern, if the term has any meaning at all; and they will surely not, as he sometimes seem to assume, remain confined to the First World. Computer games already have a thriving market in the Third. Here too, as with television, the arrival of novel kinds of connexion and simulation will tend to unify rather than divide the urban centres of the coming century, even across vast differences in average incomes. So long as the system of capital prevails, each new advance in the industry of images increases the radius of the postmodern. In that sense, it can be argued, its global dominance is virtually foreordained.

Jameson's own demonstration proceeds at another level: for him, as always, the proof of the pudding is in the cultural practices themselves. The salience of a postmodern that is no longer occidental can be judged from exemplary works of the periphery. The modernist format of Gide's *Counterfeiters*, and its moral resolution, serve as benchmarks for their startling contemporary transformation in Edward Yang's *Terrorizer*, and its relation to the new wave films in Taiwan that form, in Jameson's view, 'a linked cycle more satisfying for the viewer than any national cinema I know (save perhaps the French

[51] *Gargantua – Manufactured Mass Culture*, London 1997, pp. 6–7, 10–11, 75–77, 214, 230–231.

productions of the 20s and 30s)'. In not dissimilar fashion, Brecht's conception of *Umfunktionierung* becomes itself unpredictably retooled in the 'dignified hilarity' of Kidlat Tahimik's *Perfumed Nightmare*, where the standard oppositions of cultural nationalism – First and Third Worlds, old and new – are battered out of shape into ramshackle composites, as ingeniously serviceable as the Filipino jeepney itself.[52]

It would be hard to think of sympathies less Eurocentric than these, or more congruent with Wollen's concerns. In fact, the Zairois painters or Nigerian musicians with whom *Raiding the Icebox* concludes, creative devisers of a 'para-tourist art' inseparable from the effects of postmodern travel, teach the same lesson: that 'the choice between an authentic nationalism and a homogenizing modernity will become more and more outmoded'.[53] The final emphasis in both critics is the same: symptoms of sterility and provincialism in the metropolis, notations of imaginative renewal in the periphery. The postmodern may also signify this. 'It is because in late capitalism and in its world system even the center is marginalized', writes Jameson, that 'expressions of the marginally uneven and unevenly developed issuing from a recent experience of capitalism are often more intense and powerful', and 'above all more deeply symptomatic and meaningful than anything the enfeebled center still finds itself able to say'.[54]

Politics

Uneven development: symptomatic meaning. These are terms of art which bring us to a final crux in Jameson's work. At the

---

[52] *The Geopolitical Aesthetic – Cinema and Space in the World System*, London 1992, pp. 120, 211.

[53] *Raiding the Icebox*, pp. 197, 202–204.

[54] *The Geopolitical Aesthetic*, p. 155. Jameson's comments on the vacuity of high metropolitan forms in North America, and more widely in the First World, have been consistently – on occasion, it might be argued, even unduly – sharp. See, as examples, his interview in *Left Curve*, No 12, 1988; 'Americans Abroad: Exogamy and Letters in Late Capitalism', in Steven Bell et al. (eds), *Critical Theory, Cultural Politics and Latin American Narrative*, Notre Dame 1991; introduction to *South Atlantic Quarterly* special issue on postmodernism in Latin America, Summer 1993.

head of his first major book, *Marxism and Form*, there reads an epigraph from Mallarmé: '*Il n'existe d'ouvert à la recherche mentale que deux voies, en tout, où bifurque notre besoin, à savoir, l'esthétique d'une part et aussi l'économie politique*'.[55] Reiterating it once again in *Postmodernism* as the very emblem of his enterprise, Jameson glossed the dictum as a 'perception shared by both disciplines of the immense dual movement of a plane of form and a plane of substance'[56] – the hidden concord of Hjelmslev and Marx. The sense in which Jameson's oeuvre can be seen as a culmination of the Western Marxist tradition has been indicated above. The long suit of that tradition was always aesthetic, and Jameson has played an extraordinary hand with it. But underlying the aesthetic enquiries of this line of thinkers, of course, there was always a set of economic categories derived from *Capital* that informed their focus and direction. The work of a Lukács or Adorno is unthinkable without this constant, immanent reference. At the same time, the tradition itself produced no significant development in the field of political economy as Marx – or Luxemburg or Hilferding – understood it. Here it relied on an intellectual legacy it did not extend. An alternative classical tradition, that did seek to pursue Marxist economic analysis into the era of the Great Depression, was generally ignored. By the end of the Second World War, this line itself had lapsed.

Thus when, twenty years later – at the height of the postwar boom – Jameson was starting to write, the divorce between the aesthetic and economic dimensions of a culture of the left was at its widest. His own work took up the great aesthetic tradition. But when the economic tradition revived at the start of the seventies, as world capitalism began its slide into a long recessive wave, it is striking how actively and creatively he responded to it. The decisive role of Ernest Mandel's *Late Capitalism* in stimulating his turn towards a theory of postmodernism has already been noted. This was no stray influence. In *The Cultural*

---

[55] 'Magie', *Oeuvres*, Paris 1945, p. 399. Jameson renders this as: 'Only two paths stand open to mental research: aesthetics, and also political economy' (*Postmodernism*, p. 427), which omits the crucial 'where our need divides'.
[56] *Postmodernism*, p. 265.

Turn, Jameson has notably developed his account of the postmodern through an original appropriation of Giovanni Arrighi's *Long Twentieth Century*, whose synthesis of Marx and Braudel offers the most ambitious interpretation of the overall history of capitalism attempted to date. Here the dynamic of finance capital on the 'plane of substance' releases a movement of fragmentation on the 'plane of form', traceable all the way from the filmic preview to postmodern collages of the commonplace. In each case, the economic referent functions not as an external support, but as an internal element of the aesthetic construction itself. The final text in the same volume, 'The Brick and the Balloon', hints at a way David Harvey's *Limits to Capital* could play a not dissimilar role.[57]

Mallarmé's two paths are thus rejoined. But if the objective is a continuation of Marx's project into a postmodern world, are the aesthetic and economic the exclusive lines of march? Where does this leave the political? Its trace is not forgotten in the motivating dictum. Mallarmé speaks, after all, not of economics, but of political economy. This canonical term, however, is less unequivocal than it seems. Originally designating the classical systems of Smith, Ricardo and Malthus, it was precisely the object of Marx's critique; but when the neo-classical theories of Walras, Jevons and Menger became established as orthodoxy, with the marginalist revolution, Marx himself was assimilated to the predecessors with whom he had broken, as so many fossils of the pre-history of the discipline – the critique of political economy becoming no more than its dogmatic last chapter. In reaction, later Marxists would often claim the tradition as indeed their own, in opposition to the formalism of 'pure' economics codified by the heirs of the neo-classical thinkers. But as such, it remained a residual category – 'political' only in so far as it exceeded the calculus of the market, towards a social reference otherwise left indeterminate. This weak sense was never sufficient to define Marx's particular legacy.

But if the poetic adage leaves no independent space for the political, this figures prominently elsewhere, in the title of

---

[57] *The Cultural Turn*, pp. 136–144 ff., 184–185 ff.

Jameson's most systematic theoretical work in the field of literature itself. *The Political Unconscious* opens with the words: 'This book will argue the priority of the political interpretation of literary texts. It conceives of the political perspective not as some supplementary method, not as an optional auxiliary to other interpretive methods current today – the psychoanalytic or the myth-critical, the stylistic, the ethical, the structural – but as the absolute horizon of all reading, and all interpretation'. Jameson notes that this position will seem extreme. But its meaning is spelt out a few pages later, with the declaration: 'There is nothing that is not social and historical – indeed, everything is "in the last instance" political'.[58] This is the comprehensive sense of the term that gives its force to the book's title. Within the interpretive strategy to which it proceeds, however, there is another and lesser space of the political, understood in a more restrictive sense. In this mode Jameson argues that there are 'three concentric frameworks which mark out the sense of the social ground of a text, through the notions, first of political history, in the narrow sense of punctual event and chronicle-like happenings in time; then of society, in the now already less diachronic and timebound sense of a constitutive tension and struggle between social classes; and, ultimately, of history now conceived in its vastest sense of the sequence of modes of production and the succession and destiny of the various human social formations, from prehistoric life to whatever far future history has in store for us'.[59]

Here there is a clear hierarchy, running from the fundamental to the superficial: economic → social → political. In the latter, 'history is reduced' – the verb indicates what is likely to follow – to 'the diachronic agitation of the year-to-year, the chronicle-like annals of the rise and fall of political regimes and social fashions, and the passionate immediacy of struggles between historical individuals'.[60] What this recalls, perhaps more than anything else, is Braudel's description of *l'histoire événementielle* in his famous tier of historical times – that evanescent foam of episodes

[58] *The Political Unconscious*, pp. 17, 20.
[59] *The Political Unconscious*, p. 75.
[60] *The Political Unconscious*, pp. 76–77.

and incidents which he compared to the surf on the waves from Africa, breaking immemorially on the shores of Bahia under the faint light of the stars. The formal similarities between the two tripartite schemas, adjusting for the geographical rather than economic emphasis of *l'histoire immobile*, are evident enough. What they seem to share is a reserve towards the political conceived in a strong sense – that is, as an independent domain of action, pregnant with its own consequences.

In Braudel's case, this reticence is coherent with the whole structure and programme of his work. In the case of a Marxist, it might be doubted whether this could be so. Jameson, however, has offered reasons why it might be. In the most calculatedly shocking of his texts, he suggests a natural kinship between one of the most extreme versions of neo-liberalism – the universal modelling of human behaviour as utility-maximization by the Chicago economist Gary Becker – and socialism, in so far as both do away with the need for any political thought. 'The traditional complaint about Marxism that it lacks any autonomous political reflection', he writes, 'tends to strike one as a strength rather than a weakness'. For Marxism is not a political philosophy, and while 'there certainly is a Marxist practice of politics, Marxist political thinking, when it is not practical in that way, has exclusively to do with the economic organization of society and how people cooperate to organize production'. The neo-liberal belief that in capitalism only the market matters is thus a close cousin of the Marxist view that what counts for socialism is planning: neither have any time for political disquisitions in their own right. 'We have much in common with the neo-liberals, in fact virtually everything – save the essentials!'.[61]

Behind the buoyant provocation of these lines lies a conviction of principle – it is no accident Mallarmé's formula reappears just here.[62] But they also correspond to a sense of immediate

---

[61] *Postmodernism*, p. 265.

[62] For Jameson's fullest meditation on Mallarmé's dictum, and its effects for conceptions of politics, see his interview in the Cairene journal *Alif*, 'On Contemporary Marxist Theory', No 10, 1990, pp. 124–129, after a course taught in Egypt.

It should be said that Mallarmé himself is not to be reduced to the dichotomy of *Magie*. During the Mac-Mahon crisis of 1876–77, when the constitution of the Third Republic hung in the balance, he published an article in *La République des*

priorities. Returning to his tripartite scheme at the end of *The Geopolitical Aesthetic*, Jameson remarks of Tahimik's film that what is instructive about it is 'the way in which here the economic dimension has come to take precedence over a political one which is not left out or repressed, but which is for the moment assigned a subordinate position and role'. For this is a general lesson of the time. In the present conjuncture, of post-modernity, 'our most urgent task will be tirelessly to denounce the economic forms that have come for the moment to reign supreme and unchallenged' – 'a reification and commodification

---

Lettres declaring that 'nothing less than the sovereignty of the people' was at stake, under the rubric of – indeed – *La Politique*. For the text, see P.S. Hambly, 'Un article oublié de Stéphane Mallarmé', *Revue d'Histoire Littéraire de la France*, January–February 1989, pp. 82–84. It was in this – intensely eventful – context that he issued the famous ringing statement: 'The participation of a hitherto ignored people in the political life of France is a social fact that will honour the whole of the close of the nineteenth century. A parallel is found in artistic matters, the way being prepared by an evolution which the public with rare prescience dubbed, from its first appearance, intransigent, which in political language means radical and democratic' (in 'The Impressionists and Edouard Manet', September 1876). Two decades later, it was the Panama crisis of 1893 that set the stage for Mallarmé's return to political commentary with the text that became *Or*, the first of 'Grands Faits Divers' collected in *Divagations*, of which *Magie* was the second in time, from the same year. Both breathe an indomitable aversion to the fetishism of finance, the alchemy of speculation. *Fumée le milliard, hors le temps d'y faire main basse: ou, le manque d'éblouissement voire d'interêt accuse qu'élire un dieu n'est pas pour le confiner à l'ombre des coffres de fer et des poches – La pierre nulle, qui rêve l'or, dite philosophale: mais elle annonce, dans la finance, le futur crédit, précédant le capital ou le réduisant à l'humilité de monnaie!* – see *Oeuvres*, pp. 398, 400. [A billion is smoke, beyond the time to get your hands on it: or, the lack of bedazzlement even of interest indicates that a god is not elected to be confined to the shadow of iron coffers and pockets – The stone is null which dreams of gold, called philosophical: but it announces in finance a future credit, preceding capital and reducing it to the humility of cash!] Topical thoughts indeed, that could all but head Jameson's penultimate essay in *The Cultural Turn*.

When Mallarmé came to write his series of articles 'Variations sur un Sujet' in *La Revue Blanche* during 1895, Dreyfus had been sentenced and the political clouds of the Affair were gathering. By now his disillusion with the Opportunist parliamentary regimes of the time was complete. *Jaunes effondrements de banques aux squames de pus et le candide camelot apportant à la rue une réforme qui lui éclate en la main, ce répertoire – à défaut, le piétinement de Chambres où le vent-coulis se distrait à des crises ministérielles – compose, hors de leur drame propre à quoi les humains*

that have become so universalized as to seem well-nigh natural and organic entities'.[63] Even the politics of national liberation itself can only be inscribed in this larger battle.

Jameson's theoretical programme – we might call it, in honour of its epigraph, a materialist symbolism – has thus been formidably consistent. Its coherence can be verified *a contrario* by the one significant absence in its appropriation of the Western Marxist repertoire. For that tradition was not without a supremely political moment. Antonio Gramsci is the one great name substantially missing from the roll-call of *Marxism and Form*. In part, that is no doubt due to the sidelong position of Italy in Jameson's imposing usufruct of the resources of European culture as a whole, where France, Germany and England are the lands of reference. But it is also that Gramsci's work,

---

sont aveugles, le spectacle quotidien – see *Oeuvres*, p. 414. [Yellow collapses of banks with scales of pus and the candid hawker bringing to the street a reform that bursts in his hand, this repertory – or failing that, the stalling of Assemblies where wafts of air distract themselves with Ministerial crises – composes, beyond their own drama to which humans are blind, the daily spectacle.] The text from which this passage comes, *La Cour* ('pour s'aliéner les partis'), is the most revealing of Mallarmé's interventions of that year – a remarkable example of the fusion of 'aristocratic' and 'proletarian' motifs in the avant-garde culture of the time. To gauge the import of Mallarmé's articles in *La Revue Blanche*, it is necessary to remember their context. They appeared in the same issues of the journal, not just with drawings by Toulouse, Vallotton or Bonnard, but side by side with laudatory articles on Bakunin, Herzen, Proudhon and Marx – a celebratory review by Charles Andler on the publication of the Third Volume of *Capital*; not to speak of an eleven-part serialization of the memoirs of the *enragé* General Rossignol, Hébertiste commander in the suppression of the Vendée, honoured with a heroic representation by Vuillard. See *La Revue Blanche*, 1895, VIII, pp. 175–178, 289–299, 391–395, 450–454; IX, pp. 51–63, etc.; and for the first note on Dreyfus, attacking his 'ingenious torturers on Devil's Island', see VIII, p. 408.

A careful study of Mallarmé's political development has yet to be written. The belated publication of a substantial section of Sartre's projected work on the poet, dating from 1952, suggests what we have missed: see 'L'Engagement de Mallarmé', *Obliques*, No 18–19, 1979, now available as *Mallarmé – La Lucidité et sa Face d'Ombre*, Paris, 1986. The disappearance of the full manuscript must be accounted a major loss. The fragment that survives makes it clear that this would in all probability have been Sartre's true biographical *chef d'oeuvre*: richer in detail and sharper in focus than his subsequent account of Flaubert.
[63] *The Geopolitical Aesthetic*, p. 212.

the product of a Communist leader in prison, reflecting on the defeat of one revolution and the ways to possible victory of another, does not fit the bifurcation of the aesthetic and economic. It was eminently political, as a theory of the state and civil society, and a strategy for their qualitative transformation. This body of thought is by-passed in Jameson's extraordinary resumption of Western Marxism.

Who can say that his intuition was wrong? The grandeur of the Sardinian is stranded today, amid the impasse of the intellectual tradition he represented, plain for all to see. The current of history has passed elsewhere. If the legacies of Frankfurt or Paris or Budapest remain more available, it is also because they were less political – that is, subject to the 'contingencies and reversals' peculiar to *l'histoire événementielle* as Jameson has seen it.[64] The purification of Western Marxism to the aesthetic and economic has, as things stand, been vindicated. The theory of postmodernism as the cultural logic of late capitalism is its dazzling issue. Yet at the same time, precisely here the forclusion of the political poses a paradox. Jameson construes the postmodern as that stage in capitalist development when culture becomes in effect coextensive with the economy. What is the appropriate stance, then, of the critic within this culture? Jameson's answer rests on a three-fold distinction. There is taste, or opinion, that is a set of subjective preferences – in themselves of little interest – for particular works of art. Then there is analysis, or the objective study of 'the historical conditions of possibility of specific forms'. Finally there is evaluation, which involves no aesthetic judgements in the traditional sense, but rather seeks to 'interrogate the quality of social life by way of the text or individual work of art, or hazard an assessment of the political effects of cultural currents or movements with less utilitarianism and a greater sympathy for the dynamics of everyday life than the imprimaturs and indexes of earlier traditions'.[65]

Jameson, while avowing some personal enthusiasms as a consumer of contemporary culture, sets no special store by

---

[64] Ibid.
[65] *Postmodernism*, p. 298 ff.

them. The task of historical and formal analysis, on the other hand, has been the major part of his work as a theorist and critic – most systematically articulated in *The Political Unconscious*. What then of evaluation? If we look at *Postmodernism*, what we find are unforgettable etchings of the quality of life in this historical form, with 'its internal quotient of misery and the determinate potentiality of bodily and spiritual transfiguration it also affords, or conquers'.[66] But of calibration of the 'political effects of cultural movements', there is significantly less. The New Social Movements do figure, as a now standard *topos*, in Jameson's survey of the postmodern, where they are viewed with sympathy, but also a wary caution against inflated claims made on their behalf. But their invocation is without detail or differentiation, perhaps because they are not in the first instance – as their name implies – cultural movements *stricto sensu* at all. A more apposite case is offered by the anti-institutional conceptualism represented by artists like Haacke, whose strategy of 'undermining the image by way of the image itself' is captured graphically, if briefly.[67] But this is a relatively isolated reference, that only tends to underline the fact that there are not many others.

But is not this, it might be asked, a fair reflection of the actual paucity of oppositional – or indeed many positional – cultural movements in the postmodern? Certainly, the eclipse of organized avant-gardes, and the decline of class politics that constitutes its wider historical background, are powerfully registered by Jameson in these same pages. But they seem insufficient in themselves – for neither are absolutes – to explain the distance between promise and delivery. Here some deeper difficulty may be at work. Jameson's marriage of aesthetics and economics yields a wondrous totalization of postmodern culture as a whole, whose operation of 'cognitive mapping' acts – and this is its intention – as a placeholder of dialectical resistance to it. But its point of leverage necessarily remains in that sense outside the system. Inside it, Jameson was more concerned to monitor than to adjudicate. At this level, he has consistently warned of

[66] *Postmodernism*, p. 302.
[67] *Postmodernism*, p. 409.

the dangers of too easy denunciation of specific forms or trends, as pitfalls of a sterile moralism. That did not mean, in the other direction, any concessions to populism, for which Jameson has never had much inclination. There, his rebuke to cultural studies can be taken as a general motto: 'The standardization of consumption is like a sound barrier which confronts the euphoria of populism as a fact of life and a physical law at the upper reaches of the system'.[68]

Still, it remains true that *Postmodernism* contains no sustained attack on any specific body of work or movement within the culture it depicts, in the conventional sense of the term. In part, this is no doubt a question of psychic economy – this sort of thing has anyway never much attracted Jameson's energies; from each according to their temperament. But that there is also a theoretical issue at stake can be seen, perhaps, from a significant tension – very unusual in this writer – in Jameson's handling of a theme of central importance to his thought: namely, utopian longing. The oscillation, pointed out by Peter Fitting, is this.[69] On the one hand, he has insisted – it is one of his most daring and distinctive themes – that utopian impulses are inherently at work in the reified products of mass commercial culture too, since these 'cannot be ideological without at one and the same time being implicitly or explicitly utopian as well; they cannot manipulate unless they offer some genuine shred of content as a fantasy bribe to the public about to be so manipulated' – a bribe that will consist in some figuration, no matter how distorted or buried, of a redeemed collective order. This function Jameson terms their 'transcendent potential – that dimension of even the most degraded type of mass culture' which remains 'negative and critical of the social order from which, as a product and a commodity, it springs'.[70] The films which illustrate the argument are *Jaws* and *The Godfather*.

On the other hand, representations of utopia proper in high culture – from More to Platonov to LeGuin – are invariably held to demonstrate that this is just what we cannot imagine.

---

[68] 'On Cultural Studies', *Social Text*, No 34, 1993, p. 51.
[59] Paper at conference on postmodernism held at Changsha, Hunan, in June 1997.
[70] *Signatures of the Visible*, p. 29.

'Utopia's deepest subject' turns out to be 'precisely our inability to conceive it, our incapacity to produce it as a vision, our failure to project the Other of what is, a failure that, as with fireworks dissolving back into the night sky, must once again leave us alone with *this* history'.[71] This impotence, Jameson insists, is constitutional. What mass culture can intimate, utopian fiction cannot embody. Is there a common measure between *Independence Day* and *Chevengur*, or is this an aporia? The most relevant point, perhaps, lies elsewhere. No political criterion is given for discriminating between different figurations of utopian longing, either in commercial disguise or in prophetic imagination. But how can such forms be separated from their substance – the shape of a political dream? Can judgements between them be avoided? Here, posed in its most acute form, is the more general problem raised by the positioning of the postmodern between aesthetics and economics.

For missing in this bifurcation is a sense of culture as a battlefield, that divides its protagonists. That is the plane of politics, understood as a space in its own right. We do not have to yield to sectarian temptations within Marxism, or overheated conceptions of an avant-garde, to realize this. Such an understanding goes back to Kant, for whom philosophy itself was constituted as a *Kampfplatz* – a notion in the air of the German Enlightenment, whose military theorization came a generation later in Clausewitz. It was a major thinker of the Right who gave consequent expression to this emphasis in the field of politics. Schmitt's definition of the political as inseparable from a division between friend and foe is, of course, not exhaustive. But that it captures an ineliminable dimension of all politics is scarcely to be doubted; and it is that sense of the political which bears on the culture of the postmodern. To recall this is not to summon any intrusion. The aesthetic and the political are certainly not to be equated or confused. But if they can be mediated, it is because they share one thing in common. Both are inherently committed to critical judgement: discrimination between works of art, forms of state. Abstention from criticism, in either, is subscription. Postmodernism, like modernism, is a

---

[71] *The Ideologies of Theory*, Vol 2, p. 101.

field of tensions. Division is an inescapable condition of engagement with it.

Just this can be seen from Jameson's texts since *Postmodernism*, as the inflexion of his writing on the postmodern has become steadily sharper. For what they trace is, in effect, an involution. Postmodernism, Jameson now suggests, can already be periodized. After its first creative release in the seventies – that 'thunderous unblocking of energies', of whose relief he originally wrote[72] – there has followed a perceptible regression in the most recent period, delineated in the essays on the 'End of Art' and 'Transformations of the Image' in *The Cultural Turn*. On the one hand, the postmodern release from the bonds of the modern Sublime ('dwelling among dead monuments'), originally an emancipation, has tended to degenerate into a new cult of the Beautiful, that represents a 'colonization of reality generally by spatial and visual forms' that is also 'a commodification of that same intensively colonized reality on a world scale'.[73] With this degraded aestheticism, art appears to sink back once again into a culinary condition. At the same time, the intellectual liberation wrought with the coming of Theory, as a break-down of barriers between ossified disciplines and the emergence of more ambitious and unexpected styles of thought, has undergone a regression too. For the latest phase has seen a reinstatement of all the outdated autarchies that the de-differentiating impulses of postmodernism sought to sweep away, starting with ethics and aesthetics themselves.

Such recidivism, for Jameson, is not irreversible: the postmodern spirit could take other turns. But if we ask ourselves what the cultural slide he criticizes might correspond to, the answer is chronologically clear. When Jameson first started writing about postmodernism in the early eighties, the regimes of Reagan and Thatcher were already setting the pace in the West, the USSR was in the last throes of Brezhnevism, and national liberation a fading memory in most of the Third World. But the world-wide triumph of capitalism was still to come. Even as he finished *Postmodernism*, at the threshold of the nineties, the

---

[72] *Postmodernism*, p. 313.
[73] See *The Cultural Turn*, p. 87.

Soviet state still nominally existed. It is the complete extinction of the Communist alternative, its virtual deletion from the historical record, followed by the relentless advance of neo-liberalism through the Third World, eliminating one vestige of economic autonomy after another – a process now rolling through the last bastions of East Asia itself – that forms the background to Jameson's now more uncompromising tone. The ideological themes of the end of history, the halting of time at the bourne of liberal capitalism, become the object of a detotal-izing irony in the magnificent 'Antinomies of Postmodernity' (1994), with its redesign of Kantian categories for our contem-porary enlightenment; and then more directly again in 'End of Art – End of History?' itself (1996), which coolly switches the line of Kojève and Fukuyama to an unscheduled terminus.[74] Other texts sound the 'state of the debt' to Marx. A major work on Brecht will be with us soon.[75]

These statements are political interventions at full tilt. In the past, Jameson's writing was sometimes taxed with being insuf-ficiently engaged with the real world of material conflicts – class struggles or national risings – and so held 'unpolitical'. That was always a misreading of this unwaveringly committed thinker. Here, we have noted a theoretical reserve towards the 'eventful' that could lead to historical totalization without punctual divisions in the cultural arena – traceable, certainly, to a disinclination to yield autonomy to the political, but the opposite of its abnegation: rather its absorption into the very shape of the totality itself. This has shifted, towards greater *triage*. But considerations like these refer inwards, to the prob-lems of cultural theory as such. In the larger relationship of this body of writing to the outward world, Jameson's voice has been without equal in the clarity and eloquence of its resistance to the direction of the time. When the Left was more numerous and confident, his theoretical work kept a certain distance from immediate events. As the Left has become increasingly isolated and beleaguered, and less capable of imagining any alternative

---

[74] See *The Cultural Turn*, pp. 50–72 and 73–92.
[75] See 'Marx's Purloined Letter', *New Left Review*, No 209, January–February 1995; and *Brecht and Method* (forthcoming), London–New York 1998.

to the existing social order, Jameson has spoken ever more directly to the political character of the age, breaking the spell of the system:

> with what violence benevolence is bought
> what cost in gesture justice brings
> what wrongs domestic rights involve
> what stalks
> this silence

Index

INDEX